Stan Edwards

Christmas

D0325948

THE SECOND-LUCKIEST PILOT

THE SECOND-LUCKIEST PILOT

ADVENTURES IN MILITARY AVIATION

D. K. Tooker

NAVAL INSTITUTE PRESS
Annapolis, Maryland

Naval Institute Press
291 Wood Road
Annapolis, MD 21402
© 2000 by D. K. Tooker

All rights reserved. No part of this book may be reproduced or
utilized in any form or by any means, electronic or mechanical,
including photocopying and recording, or by any information
storage and retrieval system, without permission in writing from
the publisher.

Library of Congress Cataloging-in-Publication Data
Tooker, D. K., 1926–
    The second-luckiest pilot : adventures in military aviation /
D. K. Tooker.
        p.   cm.
    ISBN 1-55750-821-6 (alk. paper)
    1. Air pilots, Military—United States Biography. 2. Survival
after airplane accidents, shipwrecks, etc. I. Title.
UG626.T657 2000
629.13'09—dc21   99-54722

Printed in the United States of America on acid-free paper ⊗
07 06 05 04 03 02 01 00   9 8 7 6 5 4 3 2
First printing

Chapter 1 is an adapted version of "I'm the Second-Luckiest
Pilot Alive," which appeared in *Reader's Digest,* October 1967.

Unless noted otherwise, all photographs are from the author's
personal collection.

To my aviator friends who flew with me and have completed their final landings

Contents

Preface

THE FIRST THING people always ask after reading one of my stories is, "Is that really true?" I must state here that each story is totally true. Some of the dialogue is contrived, but only to express the emotion and feelings of those involved at the time.

The World War II and Korean War episodes were all written after thorough interviews with the surviving participants. Taking notes at the time and then not losing them through the years have been of immeasurable value. With one exception I have personally known each player in every story. The exception was Ens. Jesse Brown, but I was one of the airborne pilots covering the attempt to rescue him. All of the others served with me in the U.S. Navy or in various Marine Corps squadrons.

Regarding the title chapter, it is hard to describe, unemotionally, how I was rescued 760 miles at sea by a navy destroyer escort whose skipper did not expect to find a pilot down in the 62-degree water because he hadn't been told to search for one. Yes, that *is* luck; but what about another pilot who, the very next day, hit the water from fifteen thousand feet at more than a hundred miles an hour *with his chute unopened* . . . and lived?

Col. Ken Reusser, who stars in three chapters, served as best man at my wedding, as did I at his. This book chronicles his first and last combat missions, along with one in the middle for which he received the Navy Cross.

The saga of "Iwo Jima" MacSweeny was the most fun to

write. His first flight was unusual, to say nothing of its being nearly fatal. His colorful retelling of his misadventure was a thing of beauty. Besides learning to fly at the Navy's Primary Flight Training Center, he also became a semipolished professional speaker, playing all the roles in describing his misdeed.

A personal story demonstrates that some aviation mishaps can be pretty funny after the fact, particularly when the comedians are two very lucky neophyte pilots trying to fly their relatively unequipped Piper Cub from Jacksonville, Florida, all the way to California.

Other chapters deal with such exploits as landing a fighter aboard a bouncing carrier with only one arm. In another, an Air Races pilot bails out of a fighter on fire and experiences the effects of hitting the aircraft's tail on the way down. Elsewhere the author and his wife as copilot share an exciting emergency landing after an engine failure over the mountains. There is another even more exciting engine-failure adventure: Can the pilot avoid crashing in downtown Salem, Oregon? How about the farmhouse dead ahead with less than fifty feet of altitude left?

Helicopters get their just due, too. Readers will meet a pilot who owes his life to a chopper crew who rescued him from enemy hands in Korea, not once but *twice*.

Not insignificantly, the reader may also learn something about how military careers are made, saved, or lost, in sharing a helicopter experience that splits the narrow difference between "authorized" and "unauthorized."

An ALTERNATIVE title for this book could well be *Survival of the Luckiest,* with apologies to Darwin. Flying, particularly military flying, is a dangerous profession in which Lady Luck teaches us, over and over, that unpredictable factors can kill the best and the worst pilots with terrible impartiality. Blind luck plays a role so often that most pilots, especially combat pilots, come to believe that skill alone may not be enough. I was amazingly lucky, to be sure. For some others, though, luck approached the miraculous in terms of things that couldn't have happened that happened anyway.

Looking back, I acknowledge that my aviation career of some forty years was everything I ever wanted it to be; and yes, I'd do it all over again if I could.

The Second-Luckiest Pilot

1 The Second-Luckiest Pilot

ow could this be happening? Only a few seconds ago I had been sitting comfortably in the cockpit of my supersonic F-8 Crusader jet fighter en route from California to Hawaii, on the first leg of an eighteen-plane trans-Pacific flight to Japan. Suddenly, the plane was on fire and spinning violently. It was jerking and shuddering, and my head was bouncing off each side of the canopy like a ping-pong ball. And I had no idea of what had gone wrong!

On that June morning in 1963 we had just made a refueling rendezvous with a group of KC-130 tankers. The weather was beautiful, with a very slight headwind and a low cloud cover too far below to bother us at our twenty-thousand-foot refueling altitude. I was the leader of the second group of six single-seat Crusader jets from Marine All Weather Fighter Squadron 323, and we had met the KC-130s right on schedule. Just aft of the tankers, we leveled off and opened up our formation as each fighter eased up behind its respective fuel drogue.

I

Everyone had plugged in on the first stab. The green light on my console blinked on, signifying that fuel was flowing from the tanker.

I could see someone taking pictures from the big plane's rear observation window. *Poor guy,* I thought. *It must be pretty dull for him in there, watching us have all the fun.* (Later I learned he was a young lieutenant ground officer from Camp Pendleton, just along for the ride.) It was a shame that he couldn't see my confident smile hidden behind the oxygen mask. Even my flashing daredevil eyes were obscured by the darkly tinted visor lens, locked in the down position.

The first group of fighters, led by the commanding officer, Lt. Col. Claude Barnhill, had found the tankers with no strain. Each pilot had engaged his refueling probe with a tanker's trailing "basket," allowing the JP-5 jet fuel to flow under pressure from the special oversize tanks within the KC-130s' cargo compartments. As the rubberized fuel cells within the Crusader's fuselage reached maximum capacity, the pilots would announce this fact to the flight leader: "Checker Two, ready," or "This is Checker Six, full," and so on, down the line, until all of the flight was topped off.

At this point the flight leader would announce: "OK, Checker Flight, unplug. We'll make a climbing 360 to the right and join up." Our six aircraft would then resume formation as they climbed back up to their cruising altitude—in this case, "flight level 400" (forty thousand feet). We had had to descend to twenty thousand feet earlier because the tankers could not operate and refuel the fighters at the higher altitude.

Barnhill's flight of six had completed the first refueling engagement without a hitch and were now headed toward their second refueling rendezvous some seven hundred miles west and closer to Hawaii, the final destination for the first

The author's F-8 Crusader takes on fuel from a KC-130 tanker seconds before the accident.

day. Tomorrow, as expected, they would fly to Wake Island for the night, refueling over the famous Island of Midway. For the two flights of six following them, things would not go so well.

Although the green light assured me that fuel was flowing nicely, I noticed that the fuel quantity gauge was moving a lot faster than I'd ever seen it move before. As it registered full, with almost a thousand gallons, I decided to wait a few moments for the other pilots to report their "ready to unplug." I would just ride awhile on the tanker's fuel.

A muffled explosion and a loud thump were the first indications of trouble. With no control input from me, the F-8 Crusader flipped up vertically on one wing and shook the forty-foot refueling hose like a kid playing crack the whip. I remember thinking, "God, don't let me hit the tanker! They'll never get out."

A quick glance at the RPM gauge told me that the jet engine was winding down—a flameout! The sudden deceleration dropped my fighter back and below the tanker, averting a midair collision.

The next ten seconds were the shortest, the longest, and the most helpless of my life. I punched the mike button.

"This is Checker One. I've had a flameout!" (Later they said my voice sounded calm.) "I may have to leave this thing."

I was already going through the restart procedures that we had all practiced a hundred times in the operational flight trainers on the ground. The sudden quiet was deafening.

"Who's had the flameout?" asked a voice on the radio.

"The major," came the answer. "He's streaming what looks like fuel."

I watched in brief fascination as my hands went through the restart motions: close the throttle all the way to the stop, deploy the ram air turbine (a small electrical generator combined with a hydraulic pump, both needed to restore electrical and hydraulic pressure to operate the flight controls). Next, check airspeed to provide the correct engine idling RPM, then come around the horn, advancing the throttle very smoothly to avoid a "hot" start. I needn't have worried about being so careful. The engine temperature gauge kept climbing rapidly, finally hitting the stop. I was sitting on an overheated engine registering well over a thousand degrees.

A shout from my section leader, Capt. T. R. Moore: "You're trailing fire for at least a mile!"

The streaming fuel behind the jet had ignited. Someone else confirmed what I could now see in the rearview side mirrors, my own little aurora borealis.

Before my mind could accept this bad news, there was another development: The Crusader snap-rolled and entered a violent spin, slamming me from one side of the cockpit to the other, even though I had tightened the shoulder straps securely. It was so violent that it actually cracked my protective helmet.

My gloved hands, not quite so fascinating now, began their spin-recovery procedures: Wing droop down (leading edge flaps), full forward stick and opposite rudder. The controls must have burned through. They were sloppy and useless. But in my mind I was still getting my aircraft back to El Toro, somehow.

The name of the game changed again as flame suddenly shot out of the intake duct. The spinning pinwheel action had ignited the burning fuel coming out of the tailpipe, and flame was coming back over the top of the cockpit canopy, only a few inches above me. (The aircraft manufacturer, Ling-Temco-Vought, had insisted that such an event would be impossible, but the photograph taken by that friendly photographer aboard the tanker clearly showed fire coming from *both* ends of the stricken fighter.) I would have to go through this stream of fire when I ejected.

By now I'd come to rely on the two busy hands operating so coolly in front of me. *Well, that's that,* I remember thinking. *It's Pacific Ocean time.* I punched the mike button again. "I'm going to eject."

I reached up and pulled the face curtain. Searing flames engulfed me as the seat propellant charge shot me out of the jet and through the blowtorch of fire. I learned immediately how hot burning jet fuel really is.

The small, steadying seat-stabilization drogue chute deployed, stopping the tumbling, and I was headed down toward the water, only 760 miles from land.

Still tightly strapped in the seat, I thought my worries were over. But no, not so. Evidently the Aerial Refueling God wasn't through with me yet, as another problem arose.

The burning jet fighter just below me was caught in a horizontal "flat" spin and was falling slightly slower than I was. It was coming closer each second, so close that I could feel the intense heat right through the soles of my flying boots.

It's got to explode any moment, I was thinking as I fell. *How ridiculous, to escape once only to be carried back into the fire.*

At that moment the main chute, set to open automatically at ten thousand feet, slowed me with a welcome jerk. The seat came free and immediately disappeared into the fireball. As I hung there in midair, the two-million-dollar jet disintegrated below.

Almost immediately I regained all the composure of a politician who has just won by a recount. I began preparing for the impending water landing. "Be familiar with your survival equipment," I had preached to pilots in my flight. "Know your parachute and how to get out of it, how to swim clear of the shroud lines."

It takes about ten minutes to descend from an altitude of ten thousand feet, and there really isn't much to do on the way down but think. I never did like the sound of "missing at sea." *They'll search, of course,* I thought, *but for how long?*

Although I knew the tankers must have gotten a pretty good fix on me, the knowledge I had gained from having spent nine years as a helicopter pilot, participating in many fruitless sea searches, was most disheartening. We rarely found anyone in the open sea. In rough waters you can fly right overhead and still not see a man in a raft. *My wife will have to be told. She'll have to tell the kids.*

Since this line of thought can undermine a man's confidence, I diverted my mind by holding a short, informal personal inventory. My flying gloves had turned a reddish purple from the ejection through the fire. My flight suit looked like a bad dream: brown in spots, with some areas missing entirely.

My knees, forearms, and wrists were painfully burned. I could feel the skin peeling off my unprotected neck. But there was no back injury from the ejection, and I would be able to swim—not the seven hundred miles back to California, perhaps, but enough to climb into the lovely little one-man raft strapped securely to my hindquarters.

The clouds hovering over the water were racing up toward me, and I remember thinking, *Couldn't it be just a little longer?* A sudden, foggy whiteness, and a moment later I hit the water like a sack of ball bearings. Regaining the surface, I unfastened the leg and chest straps of my chute harness, and presto! I was free of the shroud lines. The billowing chute was carrying them away across the water. I took the raft from its case and inflated it. Then, after several attempts, I managed to climb aboard.

Watching the parachute slowly sinking in the dark green water, I considered briefly (very briefly) taking off my inflated Mae West and diving after it. I knew it would certainly be of good use as protection from the sun, if the sun ever came out, and, more importantly, from the cold. The water (I learned later) was 62 degrees, and I already knew all about hypothermia. However, another factor canceled the parachute retrieval plan: sharks! They hadn't shown up yet, but I was sure they would (and they did).

In the next few minutes I took stock of my new home. The waves were ten to twelve feet high—not crashing, just swelling up and down, up and down. The sky was solidly overcast, as forecast in our aerology briefing, and clouds were sitting about a hundred feet above the never-ending swells. I knew the ceiling was much too low for an aerial search, and this knowledge was more than discouraging.

And just to confirm that I was in one hell of a spot, I could see tiny bubbles floating up from a small hole on the side of the raft. Even Humphrey Bogart in *The African Queen* was in better shape.

I stopped looking down into the water and concentrated on holding on to the tiny one-man raft. My flight boots touched the far end as I sat against the back side of the raft, filling up the approximately forty inches of space available. It was like sitting in a very small bathtub in cold water, only I couldn't get out and dry off.

I could keep the raft inflated through the oral inflation tube, but to reach the tube I had to get into the water. I developed a shortcut. Whenever the raft overturned, which it did regularly, I'd blow a few breaths into the tasty inflation tube and climb back aboard. The burns really hurt, what with the salt water sloshing over them, not to mention the effort required to stay aboard the raft. It only took about half an hour of this unacceptable situation for me to feel a little sorry for myself.

I reviewed my survival gear. I had a loaded .38-caliber revolver, a whistle, three smoke flares, three dye markers, four pints of water, and a plastic survival kit the size of a cigarette package. The kit contained a fishing line, hooks, sinkers, and a set of waterproof instructions. *Great! I'll just throw a line over the side and haul in some wonderful delicacies of the sea. Dinner for one, and at the captain's table, too.*

Instead, I got seasick.

Then my raft overturned again, and I had to right it and climb back in. It looked like a long night coming up.

I knew it would be difficult for the refueling tankers to come below the overcast to look for me, and, even if they did, the visibility was not worth mentioning. If by some miracle they did spot me, they would not be able to land. Even an air-sea-rescue amphibian aircraft couldn't land in these swells. My only hope was that one of the tankers would sight me and drop a six-man life raft, the one with the larger, "first class" accommodations: more water, more flares, a solar still for distilling sea water, and, most particularly, a two-way radio.

The last would be my only salvation, I knew. Rescue aircraft could home in on my beacon and direct a ship to my location. Our squadron had received six such survival radios, and they had been installed in six Crusader seat pans—randomly. Ironically, when the flight equipment officer, 1st Lt. Cliff Judkins, had asked me if I wanted a radio put in my parachute seat pan, I'd said, "No, just install them as you see fit." I would review that decision for many years. Of course, every fighter pilot knows that, being invincible, he will never need a survival radio. Turns out I did—real bad!

By now, I figured I had been in the water for over an hour. My waterproof watch had stopped, of course, probably more as a result of the violent flat spin than of the water. Words, spoken to an empty sea, failed to buoy up my spirits, as I began to wonder seriously whether there would be a tomorrow.

By now the bad news would have been on the commercial radio stations, I assumed, correctly. No names, pending notification of kin; just "search under way." I hoped the news would be handled carefully when my wife and four children were informed. Up to now, I had been thinking fairly positively. I had enough water to survive maybe a couple of days, if hypothermia didn't get me, but I was already teeth-chattering cold.

If only the cloud cover would dissipate, the aircraft above might have a chance of spotting me. I couldn't have heard any aircraft overhead because of my crash helmet, which I was still wearing for whatever warmth it provided.

Then, wouldn't you know, the sharks arrived. Word had

gotten out somehow that a guy in a raft was in their neighborhood. They were small grey sharks, not aggressive, just curious. Occasionally they'd bump into the raft, gently reminding me not to let the swells toss me overboard anymore.

Somewhere around the two-hour mark I hit bottom—not the ocean bottom twelve thousand feet below, but mentally, and perhaps spiritually. Those tours of duty performing search and rescue missions were clearly on my mind. We never found anyone who had not been very close to shore. I remembered the Rickenbacker search near the end of World War II. He had had his downed crewmen in two eight-man rafts with water, some food, and a low-frequency homer, and it still took some twenty-one days to find them—in *warm* water.

I was looking down the barrel of No Tomorrow. I remember thinking how frustrating it all was. Death is something that everyone faces sooner or later, and here I was—and couldn't do a damn thing about it. Strangely, besides not being ready or wanting to die, I really wanted to know what had happened to my perfectly good jet fighter during the refueling. It certainly looked now as though I would never find out.

Suddenly, I saw several men wearing orange life vests standing on the water a few hundred yards away. Just as quickly they disappeared. It was another two or three minutes before another wave lifted the raft up and convinced me that the seasickness and the cold had not produced hallucinations. They were sailors, standing along the rail of a lovely U.S. Navy destroyer escort!

As the ship drove by, I put a dye marker in the water, lit a smoke flare, fired six rounds of .38-caliber tracer ammunition over her bow, and blew the whistle. I would have waved a hankie, but my hands were full.

"Surely they see me," I said aloud. "Why don't they turn this way?"

Standing up was out of the question. I started shouting. Then I realized they *had* spotted me—almost every man along the rail had a camera out, snapping pictures!

Someone on the quarterdeck of the destroyer was holding a loudhailer device. Lifting it, he said something I could not hear because my helmet was still on. Removing the helmet, I cupped my ears:

"Ahoy in the life raft, do you require assistance?"

I was incredulous! If I'd had a loudspeaker, I swear I'd have replied something like: "Oh, no thanks, I'm fine. I'll catch the next rescue vessel, as I'm just sitting down to dinner."

Of course, they were asking whether I was hurt and needed assistance in swimming to the ship, which had thoughtfully lowered a cargo net over the side. Since I wasn't about to attempt a hundred-yard swim in my soggy flight gear and boots, among the ever-present sharks, I decided to wait for more favorable options.

They then lowered a lovely whaleboat, after I assured them that I really did need assistance. Strong arms plucked me, along with my LeakyTiki, out of the water, and we were soon safely aboard one of the U.S. Navy's finest.

It was the USS *Koiner,* Destroyer Escort 331. The ship's other whaleboat had been smashed to bits the day before in just such a sea, on a practice man-overboard recovery drill; hence the captain's reluctance to risk his only other boat, even for me.

The security and warmth of the destroyer's sick bay were wonderful. I determined to be a stalwart hero, but the medicinal brandy they gave me came right back up, somewhat spoiling the effect. Not quite like that Humphrey Bogart movie.

The author, with life vest still inflated, is safely aboard the USS *Koiner*'s one remaining whaleboat. *U.S. Navy*

The author poses for the destroyer crew's cameras the next morning.

The author tries to find the words to thank the *Koiner*'s crew for saving his life. The ship's CO, Lieutenant Commander Stevenson, stands at right. *U.S. Navy*

The pharmacist mate bandaged me; and after several hours of hot towels and blankets, I regained normal body temperature, then went to bed and slept almost sixteen hours. The next morning, when I tried to find a way to thank the officers and men of *Koiner*, I learned that the ship had been on station as a navigational aid for both military and civilian aircraft flying overhead. It was, in fact, the only ship within hundreds of miles. The ship had had no radio contact with our planes, as the tanker commander had elected to remain on their refueling frequency to coordinate the rescue operations.

The *Koiner* had been monitoring the Guard (emergency) Channel, but no one had come up on that frequency. I changed that procedure right away.

The crew had seen some smoke in the distance and, investigating, had come upon my empty green helmet bag floating on the water. The ship, by chance only, chose a course that brought her almost right over me a little later.

What act of Providence had influenced the captain to pick that particular course? A few degrees left or right would have meant a sure miss in those conditions. The fact that that ship came close enough to spot my bobbing raft can only be described as miraculous.

Yes, I'm lucky. Every day I know it, remember it. But if you think such good fortune plays favorites, listen to this:

The very next day, another beautiful June morning, the last group of Crusaders (which had been returned to El Toro after my misfortune) bound for Hawaii in continuance of their mission had found the tankers and were plugged in, receiving fuel.

As their flight leader, Maj. Heil Van Campen, and I were talking (I from the deck of the destroyer escort), the same one-in-a-million accident happened. First Lt. Cliff Judkins, flying in the Number Six spot, was also at twenty thousand feet topping off his fuel from the KC-130 when BLAM! Another explosion and fire, again more than seven hundred miles at sea.

Judkins, however, could not get his ejection seat mechanism to work and had to bail out over the side. Supersonic jets are not designed to permit pilots to go over the side, as the knife-edged wing and tail assemblies will usually cause a fatality. But somehow Judkins missed both razor-sharp edges and finally pulled his ripcord at about fifteen thousand feet.

His luck took a vacation at this point. The chute only

streamed—it did not open! He plummeted three miles straight down and smashed into the ocean at what experts estimate must have been 110 to 115 miles an hour. The tiny pilot chute, designed only to help open the parachute, kept him in a vertical or straight position.

Now Lady Luck realized that she should have been paying more attention to the marines and their TRANSPAC effort. Judkins lit, if you can call it that, in a cloud-free circle ten to fifteen miles in diameter—the only clear area in hundreds of miles. This bit of luck allowed him to be located by circling aircraft and eventually rescued. He was an orthopedic nightmare, but alive. He had fallen farther without an unopened parachute than anyone in the known history of aviation— and *lived*.

He spent six months in the hospital recuperating, but he did recover and was able to fly again. He even had the fillings replaced that had been knocked out upon impact with the water.

So IF YOU see a couple of marines walking around avoiding black cats and throwing salt over both shoulders, you will know that one of them is the luckiest pilot alive.

Me? Well, I'm just Jud's older friend, sometimes referred to as the second-luckiest pilot.

2

Fifteen Thousand Feet
with an Unopened Chute

I wrote this story about three days after it happened. I had watched 1st Lt. Cliff Judkins through the first night after his rescue, in the dispensary of the heavy cruiser Los Angeles, burdened (per the attending navy doctor) with the terrible knowledge that he probably would not make it through the night. The battered pilot managed to describe to me, in graphic detail, the circumstances leading up to his near-fatal flight and his thoughts as he plummeted down to what he "knew" would be his death, with his unopened parachute fluttering feebly above.

He did live, and his life expectancy was further improved when, early next morning, a helicopter from the Marine Corps air station at El Toro, California, flew out on a one-way max-range rescue mission. Together we shared a memorable ride back to a navy hospital ship, the USS Haven in Long Beach, where a team of doctors was able to piece most of Jud back together.

He was in no condition to write the story of his miracu-

lous survival, so I wrote it as through his eyes. I had an idea
that some magazine publisher would be interested in it.
True magazine was interested enough to publish it and send
me a check for a thousand dollars (a lot of money in 1963),
which I split with Jud, 60:40. He got the $600 share because
lieutenants never have any money and he could not other-
wise have afforded to have his wife, Harriet, fly out from the
East Coast to be with him during his recovery and rehabili-
tation period. Jud and I are still close friends and now keep
in touch with each other via the Internet.

N THE brilliant sunlight twenty thousand feet above the
Pacific Ocean, I nudged my F-8 Crusader jet into position
behind the lumbering, deep-bellied refueling plane and
commenced the delicate task of plugging into the trailing
basket that would funnel fuel into my tanks. After a moment
of jockeying, I made the connection and matched my speed
to that of the slower tanker, about two hundred knots.

Soon my fuel gauges stirred, showing that all was well. In
the cockpit I was relaxed and confident. Looking around, I
was struck for an instant by the eeriness of the scene: Here I
was, attached, like an unwanted child, by an umbilicus to a
gargantuan mother streaking across the sky as though fleeing from some unnamed danger. Far below us, a broken layer
of clouds filtered the sun's glare that was shimmering in the
Pacific.

In my earphones I heard Major Van Campen, our flight
leader, chatting with Major Tooker, who was down below
on a destroyer. Major Tooker had parachuted into the ocean
the day before when his Crusader had flamed out mysteri-
ously during refueling and then became a ball of fire, leaving
him no choice but to eject. We all supposed it had been some

freak, one-in-a-million malfunction, and everybody in the squadron regretted the loss of that aircraft and the blemish on our otherwise perfect safety record.

"Three minutes to mandatory disconnect point," the tanker commander said. I checked my fuel gauges again: everything normal. In a few hours, I knew, we'd all be having dinner at the Kaneohe Officers Club on Oahu, Hawaii. Then, after a short overnight rest, we would continue our six-thousand-mile trek to Atsugi, Japan, via Wake Island. Our entire outfit, Marine All-Weather Fighter Squadron 323, was being transferred to the Far East for a year of operations.

My fuel gauges indicated that the tanks were full. I noticed that my throttle lever was sticking a little. Odd, because the friction lock holding it in place was loose. It grew tighter as I tried to manipulate it gently.

Then, KA-WHAM! I heard a crack-like explosion, and the Crusader nosed up into an almost vertical position. I could see the RPM gauge unwinding and the tailpipe temperature dropping. The aircraft was flaming out! I punched the mike button: "This is Jud. I've got a flameout!" Then my radio went dead; I was neither sending nor receiving anything.

Breaking the connection with the tanker, I nosed over into a shallow dive to pick up flying speed again. I needed a few seconds to think. I yanked a handle extending the air-driven emergency generator into the slipstream, hoping to get ignition for an air start along with hydraulics for the flight control system. The igniters clicked encouragingly, and the RPM indicator started to climb slowly, as did the tailpipe temperature. For one tantalizing moment I thought everything would be all right. But the RPM indicator stabilized at 30 percent capacity—not nearly enough power to maintain flight—and refused to go farther.

The fire warning light (we call it the "panic light") blinked on, and in the rearview mirror I could see fuel as it streamed from the tailpipe like water from a bucket. At the same instant, my radio came back on, powered by the emergency generator, and a great babel of voices burst through my earphones, all saying, more or less, "Jud, you're on fire, get out of there!"

Fuel pouring out of the aircraft had ignited behind me in an awesome trail of fire.

The suddenness of the disaster overwhelmed me, and I thought, *This can't be happening.* The radio voices in my ears kept urging me to pull the ejection handle and abandon the aircraft. I pressed my mike button and told the flight leader, "I'm ejecting!"

Taking my hands off the controls, I reached above my head for the canvas curtain that would start the ejection sequence. I pulled it down hard over my face and waited for the tremendous kick in the pants that would send me rocketing upward, free of the aircraft.

Nothing happened. The canopy, which was supposed to explode away and jettison, was still in place, and so was I.

My surprise lasted only a second. Then I reached down between my knees for the alternate firing handle, and gave it a vigorous pull. Nothing! My continued presence in the cockpit immobilized me with disbelief.

The plane was now in a steep 60-degree dive. For the first time, I felt panic softening the edges of my determination. I was trapped in this aircraft, and I was going to die. There was no way out. With great effort, I pulled my thoughts together and tried to imagine some solution.

A voice in my earphones was shouting: "Ditch the plane! Ditch in the ocean!" It must have come from the tanker skipper, because every jet pilot knows that you cannot ditch a jet. The plane would hit the water at too high a speed, flip over, and sink like a stone—if it didn't explode on impact.

I grabbed the stick and leveled the aircraft. Then I yanked the alternate handle again in an attempt to fire the canopy and start the ejection sequence, but still nothing happened. That left me with only one imaginable way out: jettison the canopy manually and try to jump from the aircraft without aid of the ejection seat. Was such a thing possible? I didn't know. I did know that no jet pilot had ever done it in a Crusader successfully. The massive knife-edge tail section was almost certain to strike the pilot's body and kill him before he could fall free of the aircraft. But my desperation was growing, and any scheme that offered a shred of success seemed better than riding that plane into the sea.

I jettisoned the canopy by hand, and with a great "whooosh" it disappeared from over my head. Before trying to get out, I trimmed the aircraft to fly in a kind of sideways skid: nose-high, tail swung around slightly to the right.

Then I stood up in the seat and put both arms in front of my face. I was sucked out immediately from the plane. I cringed against the expected blow from the tail section, but it never came. In an instant I knew I was out of there and free, and I waited . . . until my body, hurtling with the 250-knot momentum of the aircraft, slowed and began to fall, pulled only by gravity.

I yanked the D-ring on my parachute and braced myself against its opening. I heard a weak pop above me, but somehow my fall was unabated. I looked up and saw that the small 18-inch pilot chute had deployed. But I also saw a sight that made me shiver with disbelief and horror. The main 24-foot chute was tangled in its own shroud lines. It had not opened!

I could see the white folds, neatly arranged, fluttering use-lessly in the air.

Frantically, I shook the risers in an attempt to balloon and open the chute. It didn't work. I pulled the confused bundle of nylon down toward me and wrestled with the shroud lines, but the great streaming fingers of the parachute remained closed.

I looked down hurriedly. There was still plenty of alti-tude remaining. Frustrated and sickened with panic, I wanted everything to halt while I collected my thoughts. Through a large break in the undercast, I saw a ring of turbulence in the ocean with a white froth at its center—the point where my airplane had smashed into the sea.

Again, I shook the risers and shroud lines, but the rushing air was holding the chute tightly in its grotesque entangle-ment. The terrible realization broke over me that I had done all that I could reasonably do, and now there was nothing to do but fall. I descended for a few long seconds, staring down into the sea.

I passed through whiteness, the low clouds at perhaps fif-teen hundred feet, and then there was nothing at all between me and the ocean. I have no recollection of positioning myself properly or even bracing for the impact. In fact, I don't remember hitting the water at all. One instant I was falling, and, in the next, a shrill, high-pitched whistle hurt my ears and I was suddenly cold. In that eerie half world, I thought: *Am I alive?* And I decided, not all at once, *Yes, I think I am. I am alive.*

The water helped clear my senses, and then I was finally back at the surface after what seemed to be an eternity under water, coughing and retching. The Mae West around my waist had inflated, and I concluded that the shrill whistling sound had been gas leaving the CO_2 cylinders and filling the life vest, the toggles having been activated by the force of hitting the water. I had no idea how deep I plunged, but it had to be at least thirty or forty feet.

A sense of urgency gripped me, as though there were some task I ought to be performing. Then I knew what it was. The parachute was slowly tugging at me from under the water, billowed out now like a Portuguese man-of-war. *What a paradox,* I thought, *the chute only opens underwater.* I tried reaching down for the hunting knife in the knee pocket of my flight suit—and I knew I was badly hurt. The pain was excruciating. Was my back broken? I tried to arch it slightly and felt the pain again.

I tried moving my feet, but that, too, was impossible. They were immobile, and I could feel the bones in both ankles grating against each other.

The hunting knife had been ripped off by the water impact, but I had another smaller one in an upper pocket of my flight suit. With difficulty, I extracted it and began slashing feebly at the spaghetti-like mess surrounding me.

Finally I was free of the parachute and I commenced a tentative search for the survival pack—containing my one-man life raft, some canned water, food, fishing gear, and some dye markers—that should have been strapped to my hips. Everything was gone. It had been ripped away from the force of my hitting the water.

How long will the Mae West flotation vest sustain me? I wondered. I wasn't sure, but I knew I needed help pretty quickly. The salt water I had swallowed felt like an enormous rock in the pit of my gut. But worst of all, here I was, completely alone, some seven hundred miles from land, lolling around in the deep troughs and crests of the cold waters of the

Pacific Ocean. And my aircraft, upon which had been lavished such affectionate attention, was now thousands of feet (twelve thousand, I learned later) below, on the bottom.

At that moment, I was struck with the incredible series of coincidences that had just befallen me. I knew my misfortune had been a two-in-a-million thing, after Major Tooker's ejection of the day before. The explosion aloft, the failure of the ejection mechanisms, the streamed chute—these were accidents which, even had they occurred singly, would have been extraordinary in the face of the squadron's perfect safety record and the impeccable standards to which all our equipment conformed.

It wasn't long, ten minutes perhaps, before I heard the drone of a propeller-driven plane. The KC-130 four-engine tanker came into view, flying low. It dropped several green dye markers near me and, farther out, some smoke flares. Later I found out that I had splashed down in a clear area about ten miles in diameter, the only cloud-free area within otherwise solid overcast for hundreds of miles. I thought perhaps the Aviation God was trying to balance out the bad and good luck on his scale of fairness.

The tanker pilot circled, came in lower this time and dropped an inflated life raft about fifty yards from me. I took two strokes toward it and almost blacked out from the pain. The tanker circled again and then dropped another raft even closer, but I knew I didn't have a chance in hell of reaching it.

The water seemed to be getting colder now (62 degrees), and a chill gripped me. I looked at my watch, but the so-called unbreakable crystal was shattered and the hands torn away, leaving only the strap and empty case, witnesses to irresponsible advertising. I tried to relax and think about being rescued, but the constant movement of the twelve-foot swells was difficult to ignore. Somewhat irrelevantly, I remembered the words W. C. Fields had chosen for his epitaph: "On the whole, I'd rather be in Philadelphia."

As I pondered whether there would be a tomorrow in my future, I remembered somewhat incongruously that my ground job in the squadron was flight equipment officer, which included the duties of parachute officer. This little adventure would not look good on my fitness report.

In a little over two hours (just a guess) a coast guard amphibian plane flew over and circled as though deciding whether to land. But the huge swells were much too high, and I knew he couldn't make it. He came in extremely low and dropped another raft, this one with a 200-foot lanyard attached. The end of the cord landed barely three feet from me, and by paddling gently backward, using my arms only, I managed to reach it, then catch hold of it and pull the inflated raft to me. Without even trying, I knew I couldn't crawl into the raft, so I just took a one-armed grip over one side and hung on as best I could. It was particularly frustrating because I knew that if I could only get into the raft the oncoming hypothermia would be considerably delayed.

The coast guard amphibian made a final low pass, waggled his wings, and flew off to the west, not homeward to the east. As it turned out, he was headed toward a squadron of navy minesweepers that were returning to the United States after a tour in the Western Pacific. Unable to tune to their radio frequencies, the helo pilot had trailed a wire from the aircraft and dragged it across the bow of the lead minesweeper, the USS *Embattle*. The minesweeper captain understood this subtle plea for help, finally, and took off at top speed in the indicated direction.

In the water, I was drifting in and out of consciousness during the time it took the minesweeper to reach me. They spotted me while I was teetering on the crest of a wave. Soon its bow was pushing in toward me and I could see sailors in orange life jackets crowding along the railings. A bearded man in a black rubber suit jumped into the water and swam to me.

"Are you hurt?" he asked.

"Yes," I said. "My legs and back."

I was very cold now and worried about the growing numbness in my legs. The imminence of rescue must have made me light-headed, for I remember only vaguely being hoisted aboard the ship, laid out on deck, and having my flight suit cut away.

I'm told I screamed: "Don't touch my legs!" But I don't remember it. Somebody gave me a shot of morphine.

Later, it must have been several hours, a man was bending over me, and I could hear him asking questions. It was a doctor who had been high-lined over from a heavy cruiser, the USS *Los Angeles,* which was on its last voyage from Hawaii, to be decommissioned at the Long Beach Naval Shipyard.

As he leaned over me, he asked: "You have a long scar on your abdomen. How did it get there?"

I told him about a serious auto accident I had had four years earlier in Texas, as a result of which my spleen had been removed. He grunted and then asked more questions while he continued examining me. Then he said, "You and I are going to take a little trip. Just over to the *Los Angeles*. It's steaming alongside."

Somehow they got me into a wire stretcher and hauled me, dangling and dipping, across the watery interval between the *Embattle* and the cruiser. In the *Los Angeles*'s sick bay they gave me another shot of morphine, thank God, and started thrusting hoses into me. I could tell from all the activity and from the intense, hushed voices, that they were worried. I vaguely remembered the doctor telling Major Tooker, who had also been high-lined over from his destroyer rescue vessel, something about my kidneys not functioning and that a rescue helo was needed if I were to pull through.

My body temperature was down to 94 degrees, my intestines and kidneys in shock. The doctor and the major never left me during the night, and a corpsman took my blood pressure every 30 minutes. I was unable to sleep. Finally, a quart or more of sea water came out of me and the nausea was relieved a bit.

By listening, I pieced together the nature of my injuries: both ankles were broken, the left in five places, the right in three; a tendon in my left foot was cut; the right pelvis was fractured; number seven vertebra was fractured; I had a partial collapse of the left lung; many cuts and bruises on my face and body; and, of course, my intestines and kidneys had been impacted into complete inactivity.

The next morning, the doctor who had seen me through the night, Dr. Valentine Rhodes, told me that the Los Angeles was steaming at flank speed to a rendezvous with a helicopter two hundred miles off Long Beach, California.

Around noon I was hoisted into the belly of a Marine H-34 helicopter from the Los Angeles's fantail, and we whirred off to a hospital ship, the USS Haven, docked in Long Beach.

Once aboard the Haven, I was besieged from all sides by doctors with more needles, tubes, and X-ray machines. But their reaction to my condition was so much more optimistic than I had expected that I finally broke down and let go some tears of relief, exhaustion, and thanks.

My ankles were put back in place with the help of steel pins. The partially collapsed left lung was reinflated, and my kidneys and intestines returned to normal. I wondered whether I would ever fly jets again. I did not know, however,

The author and Clifford Judkins at the fifty-year reunion of VMF-323, held at the El Toro Officer's Club in 1993.

that I would be faced with six months of rehabilitation and therapy.

The Marine Corps discovered that the cause of my flame-out and that of Major Tooker's was the failure of the automatic pressure cutoff switches in the refueling system in the fighter's fuel cell, which is made of heavy reinforced rubber. When filled over capacity, it had simply burst like a balloon, and the fuel pouring out the tailpipe had caught fire. The problem was rectified after the U.S. Navy had grounded its entire inventory of about 350 F-8 Crusaders.

Do I feel lucky? That word doesn't describe my feelings. To survive a fifteen-thousand-foot fall with an unopened chute is a fair enough feat, and to land in the only clear spot in the ocean might possibly (but erroneously) be seen as intentional.

But here's the kicker: Dr. Rhodes told me in the sick bay of the *Los Angeles* that if I had had a spleen, it almost certainly would have ruptured when I hit the water, and I would have bled to death internally. As I had told the doctor, my spleen had been removed a few years before. Of the twenty-six pilots in our squadron, I was the only one without a spleen. Something to think about! (Lt. Cliff Judkins, as told to Maj. Donald K. Tooker)

EPILOGUE

There is precious little information on the survival rate for persons who hit the water at fifteen thousand feet without a working parachute. First Lt. Clifford Judkins is one of only a handful who have lived after falling from even much lower altitudes.

Amazingly, Judkins never lost consciousness except for a brief moment after hitting the water. He spent almost six months in naval hospitals and eventually was returned to full flight status. Jud flew the F-8 Crusader for a short time after his convalescence so as, in a manner of speaking, to "get back on the horse." He then served a full combat tour in Vietnam, leaving the military service in 1966 to become a Delta Airlines pilot. He has since retired from Delta as a captain, with a total of eighteen thousand hours, still with only that *one* attempt at parachuting.

During my last visit with Jud aboard the navy hospital ship USS *Haven* before I left for our squadron's overseas tour, he expressed his feelings regarding his recent bout with Lady Luck. He was still on morphine and kind of dopey when he said, "Major, the way things are going, if I arrived at St. Peter's Gate, heaven would probably be closed that day for inventory."

MANY YEARS LATER I learned that, as First Lieutenant Judkins lay in his bed aboard the navy hospital ship in Long Beach, he was visited by an official Marine Corps board of investigation consisting of one Marine Corps major and one second lieutenant. Their mission was to determine why First Lieutenant Judkins had lost his government-issued .38 caliber pistol and whether any culpability was involved. Judkins—three operations and ten days into his convalescence—stated emphatically that (1) he did not still possess said weapon and (2) no navy rescue personnel had taken it from him as he lay prostrate on the minesweeper's deck after his plunge into the Pacific.

After reading Judkins his rights, the two board members took copious notes and finally finished the inquisition with: "To the best of your knowledge, where is the weapon now?" His response was rude but true. "At the bottom of the God-damned ocean at about twelve thousand feet." The two investigating officers then took their leave after thoughtfully wishing the fallen pilot a speedy recovery.

Two weeks later the second lieutenant returned and asked Judkins to sign a typewritten statement about the whereabouts of the .38. He refused and told the visiting officer, "Get the hell out of here." The incident was closed, and nothing more was ever said about the loss of approximately $68 of government property, USMC type.

The interesting thing here, however, is that the U.S. Navy never questioned (beyond the routine accident investigation) the loss of their two-million-dollar jet fighter aircraft. Makes you wonder.

3 The Jesse Brown Story

Some stories are fun to write. No, most stories are fun to write; but this story, all too true, was very difficult. Although it happened almost fifty years ago, I still get choked up when I read or remember it.

I never met Jesse Brown. The only time I saw him was from the cockpit of my F4U Corsair fighter while airborne near the frozen Chosin Reservoir in December 1950. He was also sitting in the cockpit of a Corsair fighter, but he was on the ground, having crash-landed after being hit by enemy ground fire. His plane had a strange bend in it, right at the cockpit. As if this were not bad enough, the aircraft had a small but stubborn fire burning under the nose section. For some reason, he wasn't getting out. He was just sitting there.

Our marine aircraft were part of a circling force consisting of about ten fighters, including Jesse's original flight members. Together, we could hold off a flotilla of enemy aircraft, but to the bent fighter on the ground, we were of very little help.

Before this drama was over, one pilot had earned the

*Congressional Medal of Honor and a second pilot, the Silver
Star, for gallantly putting their lives on the line to help save
another.*

THE DATE was 4 December 1950. The location was twenty
miles north of the frozen Chosin Reservoir, almost to the
Yalu River itself. With temperatures at night dropping to
20 and 30 degrees below zero, it was to be the coldest winter
ever recorded in North Korea. Only a few days earlier, ten
divisions of Chinese Communist troops had walked across
the newly frozen river into North Korea and were streaming south, turning a home-by-Christmas police action into a
costly and bitter war. The business at hand was to reconnoiter
the area and provide air cover for the Army and Marine troops
cut off in their withdrawal toward the city of Hungnam.

A flight of four F4U-4 propeller-driven aircraft had taken
off earlier from the deck of the carrier USS *Leyte* (CV-32) and
were proceeding on their assigned armed reconnaissance mission. Flying at about seven thousand feet indicated (actually
fifteen hundred feet above ground level), in loose formation
behind their leader, Lt. Cdr. Dick Cevoli, the four navy pilots
were confident that their tried-and-true Corsair fighter bomb-
ers of World War II fame could handle the situation.

Behind Cevoli, Lt. (jg) Bill Koenig was flying in the Number Two spot. A career naval officer from Des Moines, Iowa,
Koenig was known to enjoy the flying but to hate the biting
cold, which in the poorly heated cockpits penetrated the
rubber anti-exposure suits and long underwear that every
pilot wore. He wondered if the small-arms fire would be as
intense as an earlier flight had reported.

Just behind Koenig, the third pilot huddled behind his
control stick, chilled to the bone. Ens. Jesse Brown, like the
others, had never experienced cold like this before. He had

In their stateroom aboard the USS *Leyte* off the Korean coast in 1950, Lt. (jg) Bill Koenig reads while Ens. Jesse Brown writes a letter home. Koenig was a member of Brown's last flight.
courtesy of William Koenig

taken his flight training at Pensacola, Florida, as a midshipman. He had received his wings in 1948 and a year later was commissioned an ensign in the Naval Reserve while aboard his carrier, the USS *Leyte*. There was one thing, however, that made this quiet, well-liked young man from Mississippi different from the rest of the flight members: He was the U.S. Navy's first Black aviator.

The fourth and last man, inevitably called "Tail-end Charlie," was Tom Hudner, a lieutenant (jg), the same as Koenig. He, too, was a career officer, a Naval Academy graduate from Fall River, Massachusetts.

As the flight wheeled slowly in a gentle arc and entered the valley leading into the Chosin Reservoir area, a burst of crimson red tracers arched across their flight path in front of them. A milky overcast sky reached down almost to the hilltops, leaving them with precious little room in which to maneuver. "Welcome to North Korea," Hudner muttered under his breath.

The mission had begun. Comments from other flights came crackling through the earphones as the pace began to quicken.

"Bogeys at ten o'clock," the flight leader advised. Cevoli knew that they were friendly aircraft but wanted the flight to be aware of their location.

"Bogeys at two o'clock low," said Koenig from his wing position on Cevoli. "They're Corsairs."

He had just spotted the flight previously pointed out by Cevoli. Indeed, they were marine Corsairs on a similar armed reconnaissance mission. Enemy foxholes and trenches were visible along the ridge tops, but it was difficult to see if they were occupied.

"Okay, Able Flight, spread out and charge your guns. We'll check these hilltops for activity," Cevoli ordered.

Each pilot acknowledged with a "Roger" and in turn placed his .50-caliber gun charger to the "ready" position. A long black scar etched in the snow dramatically registered the point where a marine pilot had been killed earlier in the day. The low cloud cover had negated any bailout possibilities, and the plane had exploded on impact as he had attempted a belly landing, his only option.

Hudner glanced at his watch for no particular reason and noted that it was 3:10 in the afternoon. The flight approached the upper end of the valley and fell into single file as they flew back down the opposite side. Jesse, in his Number Three position, added a little power as the distance between him and the Number Two man began to widen. He cupped his hands to his mouth to blow some warmth through the leather flying gloves.

Suddenly without warning, Jesse's engine began to run rough as the Corsair rapidly lost airspeed. He pressed the mike button: "This is Able Three. I think I'm hit! I' m losing power!"

For a moment he could not tell what had happened. He knew his aircraft had been hit, perhaps mortally. His RPM was winding down and his oil pressure dropping fast. The throttle response was nil. Then it was painfully apparent to Jesse that his aircraft was without power. He was flying a six-ton glider. A constant chatter of advice filled the air as he headed his disabled Corsair toward the only clearing in sight. He was already too low to bail out, as this was an era before the low-altitude ejection seat.

Cevoli reacted instinctively. He signaled for the flight to join up as he assessed Jesse's chances for a successful belly landing. *P-poor to below,* he thought, as he looked at the mountainous and snow-covered terrain.

"Able Three, the only clear spot I see is at your ten o'clock, if you can make it that far."

Jesse's "Roger" was flat and without enthusiasm.

"Able Three, can you maintain any power at all?"

"That's a negative," was Jesse's terse reply. A moment's pause, then, "I'm going in."

There were no more words to say and no more suggestions —time was up for Able Three. The remaining flight members circled, waiting as Jesse made his final approach to a small area no larger than a couple of football fields. Able Three disappeared for a moment in a shower of snow and flying debris.

No one in the flight spoke, and the other pilots on the

same frequency respected the situation by maintaining radio silence also. It was almost a minute before Cevoli broke the stillness.

"Able Two, get as much altitude as this overcast will permit. Get out a Mayday and tell 'em we've got to have a chopper. It's the only way. And tell 'em it's getting dark fast. Able Four, make a low pass over the aircraft and I'll cover you."

"Roger, from Able Four." Hudner eased the power back and started down. Now the danger from enemy ground fire seemed unimportant. Only moments before the thought of his getting hit had been foremost in his mind. Now it didn't really matter. Jesse was down, probably hurt, maybe even dead. That black scar in the snow they had just flown over was still very much in his mind.

Closing rapidly on the crash site, Hudner saw that Jesse had landed in a bowl-like depression. *Good work to land on that,* thought Hudner—but closer inspection of the freshly cut swath in the snow revealed a jagged and boulder-strewn surface. Jesse had done a magnificent job just to land upright. The Corsair's fuselage was badly bent at the cockpit and smoking slightly, and the engine and propeller were missing.

"Able Leader, I've got to make another pass. The fuselage is buckled and the canopy is closed. I can't see any signs of Jesse."

"Roger, Able Four. I'm going to switch to emergency channel for a second and get some more fighter cover in here."

Another transmission cut out the next sentence, and Hudner thought to himself about the enemy on the ground, just waiting for another low-flying target.

"This time I'll come in slower for a better look," Hudner announced as he lowered his landing flaps and glided in again toward the downed aircraft. The significance of what he saw did not immediately register: Jesse was alive. He had opened his canopy and was waving from the cockpit. But the forward portion of the aircraft was still emanating smoke, an indication of a small but steady, smoldering fire. Jesse was in an ominous predicament

"Able Leader from Able Four. The aircraft appears to be pretty much intact, but it's on fire. Jesse's alive but he's just sitting there in the cockpit; he's not getting out."

"OK, Able Four. I understand. Good work. Standby one."

Cevoli then radioed instructions to a marine flight of four Corsairs, approaching. They were to provide protective cover along the hilltops surrounding the small valley. He did not have to warn them that the small-arms fire was very accurate.

"Able Four from Able One. Is he out yet or what?"

"That's a negative, Able One. He's just sitting there." By now, Hudner had completed his third pass, this time flying both low and slowly enough to recognize Jesse's features. For several minutes no one spoke as they circled the crash scene, each attempting to visualize what was happening on the ground. The Corsair looked like a seal with a broken back.

The marines flying cover were joined by another navy flight of four Corsairs, which then formed a large eight-plane circle. These aircraft were making runs on every hilltop in their joint protective effort. Almost fifteen minutes had passed since Jesse had gone down. It was now 3:30 p.m. and getting darker.

Hudner could observe that Jesse still had not abandoned his aircraft, which was bad news. No one sits in the cockpit of an aircraft that has just crashed and is on fire unless he has no choice. The immediate news on the radio was that rescue facilities had been alerted, nothing more. The fire was no worse, but it had not gone out. It seemed to Hudner that twice, in a matter of a few minutes, time was about to run out for Jesse in Able Three. In his mind, the time for action had arrived. Someone had to do something. No order was given and no conversation preceded Hudner's decision.

"This is Able Four, I'm going in to land beside Jesse."

Cevoli's reply was a noncommittal, "Roger, we'll try to cover you."

The odds of successfully landing a fighter-bomber at over a hundred miles an hour on a mountain slope among boulders hidden by the snow were, at the very best, slim. Hudner had weighed this carefully. Assuming that he could manage to walk away in one piece from the crash landing, what options remained? Capture, most assuredly, and that possibility only if the enemy troops weren't too stirred up by all of the strafing and napalming they had been receiving.

The helicopter might show up, and then again, it might not. He knew that helicopters of that period lost power at high altitudes and were not supposed to fly after dark, but a chopper would be his only way out—if there was to be a way out. Jesse, he concluded, must be pinned in the cockpit or be too badly injured to extricate himself. The clincher was his awareness that the fire would soon reach the cockpit, raising the thought of what every pilot dreads most—being burned alive.

"Good luck, Tom," someone said. He dropped full landing flaps, leaving the landing gear up, and eased back the power to slow down in the final phase of his approach. As his plane slammed into the frozen, rock-hard ground, Lt. (jg) Thomas Hudner realized he had now placed his remaining life span into the hands of God.

FIFTEEN MILES south of the Chosin reservoir, at a tiny airstrip at Hagaru-ri, Marine 1st Lt. Charles Ward crouched next to a small oil stove trying to keep warm, unaware that he was about to play a part in one of the world's first high-altitude helicopter rescues. The helicopter was still very much in its embryonic stage, roughly equivalent to the airplane's development just prior to World War I. The helicopter was not flown at night operationally because of inadequate instrumentation. It also had very poor lifting power above five thousand feet.

Charlie Ward was a veteran of ten years of military service, four of them as a helicopter pilot. He was prematurely grey and hailed from the Deep South. His drawl was as slow as he was good-natured. Imperturbable, Charlie possessed the traits—the determination and the courage—of a perfect helicopter rescue pilot. His favorite expression was, "I don't know the meaning of the word 'fear'—not because I'm brave, I just don't understand big words."

Even the North Koreans would have liked Charlie under more favorable world conditions. He had enlisted in 1941 before Pearl Harbor and had served as a drill instructor at Parris Island boot camp in South Carolina. He had volunteered for flight training and received his wings and commission in 1943. Upon graduation, he married Margaret, his childhood sweetheart. Just before his tour in the Central Pacific in 1944, he had walked away from an SBD dive-bomber that he had "dead-sticked" into the Florida swamps after an engine failure. As Charlie told it, "The only thing left after some nine-inch diameter trees had cut through the aircraft was the cockpit and the seat with me strapped in it."

After the war, he'd joined the first marine helicopter unit, which had been formed in early 1947. He had become the tenth marine helicopter pilot to be so designated and had left the United States by carrier in September 1950 with a detachment of Sikorsky helicopters on board the USS *Leyte* bound for Korea. At Wonsan he had stood beside Bob Hope and

Marilyn Maxwell to help welcome the First Marine Division ashore during their well-advertised amphibious landing.

When rumors materialized that the Chinese Communists might join forces with the North Koreans and cross the Yalu River, Charlie's unit was dispatched to the north in anticipation of the expected heavy casualties. He was one of three helicopter pilots assigned to the forward medical station at Hagaru-ri at the southern end of the Chosin Reservoir. The previous day, 3 December, Maj. Bob Langstaff had been shot down and killed while attempting to rescue a downed pilot north of the reservoir. The detachment was now reduced to Charlie and Capt. Wally Blatt.

Their parent unit, VMO-6, was headquartered some forty miles to the south at Yonpo, a large airfield near the port of Hamhung. Of the squadron's ten original helicopters, only five remained intact.

At approximately 3:50 p.m. in a tent at Hagaru-ri, a radioman handed a message to 1st Lt. Ward. An aircraft had been shot down about twenty miles northwest of the reservoir: "Helo rescue requested. Coordinates 624-419. Expedite."

Charlie received the information calmly. He quietly instructed his crew chief to check everything over for a mountain rescue, and then he headed for the operations tent to verify the map coordinates.

"I hope they're mistaken about the location," Charlie muttered to himself. "That's above the six-thousand-foot level. That gives me about a 200-pound payload even after I've burned down some fuel. Since I weigh about 165 pounds, any pilot I'm going to rescue had better not weigh over 35 pounds."

He headed out of the operations tent and walked quickly to his helicopter. After several anxious moments, the engine finally sputtered into life. In the extreme cold it was very difficult to start the helicopter engines. The mechanics had been unable to start Captain Blatt's helicopter all day long.

"I've got everything all set, Lieutenant," the crew chief informed Charlie. "I've stuck in an extra carbine and some ammo for us."

"Fine, Sarge, thanks a lot. Only problem is, if you go, I can't bring the other guy out. It's just too high up for this ole bird. I guess you'd better wait here, and besides, you'd miss the movie tonight."

"Yes, Sir, Lieutenant." The crew chief knew there wasn't any movie. There hadn't been one since they had left the carrier. He also knew that rescuing downed pilots was a coordinated two-man operation. Lieutenant Ward would have his hands full.

"I'll keep a light in the window, Lieutenant."

"Thanks," Charlie nodded, and he lifted off, heading north by northeast.

He had further lightened his load by leaving behind the toolbox, carbine, and ammunition. He hoped this had been a wise decision. From his pilot's seat far forward in the helicopter, Charlie could see the small airstrip at Yudam-ni. He had several friends flying in and out of there. The strip was unique in that the marines owned only the southern half, while the North Koreans claimed title to the northern half. This situation always made every landing, in Charlie's words, "exciting."

A few minutes more, Charlie judged, and he should be in contact with the flight leader covering the downed pilot. It was 4:30 p.m., and the overcast sky was blocking out what little light remained. For the aircraft circling the two downed pilots, time was also running out. Cevoli and Koenig were both low on fuel. They had been airborne almost three hours and were still a long way from home.

Although they had run out of ordnance earlier, they were reluctant to leave the rescue operation. Cevoli had directed several other flights into the area to sustain their protective air cover. As darkness approached, so did the possibility of a midair collision. With too many airplanes in too small an airspace, the risk to the covering pilots milling around in the dim light was becoming unacceptable.

On the ground the situation was worse. Hudner had executed a near-perfect wheels-up belly landing. His Corsair had scraped to a stop fifty yards from Jesse's burning aircraft. He shut off all his switches and lost no time in exiting the cockpit and making his way through the snow to Jesse's plane.

"Hey, Jesse, how you doin'?"

"Boy, am I glad to see you," he replied. Jesse's face was pale from the cold and pain. Hudner noted that it was so cold it hurt to take a deep breath.

"Are you stuck in there or what?"

"Yeah, the fuselage is buckled and jammed against my leg." Jesse paused for a moment and then added, almost casually, "I can't move."

"Are you in pain, Jesse?"

"Yeah, but mainly I'm cold. I can't believe this cold!" He glanced toward the smoldering fire. Both of them knew it could not be far from the main fuel cell.

Hudner nodded his concurrence and shifted his attention from Jesse to the airplane. The fuselage was buckled in two places, not one. The engine had been torn from its mounting points, and the large four-bladed propeller lay a hundred yards away. The accessory section immediately in front of the cockpit was intact, and the fire had started inside it. The aircraft's magnesium was apparently burning and slowly eating its way aft toward the fuel tank, also just in front of the cockpit, which was literally in Jesse's lap.

Hudner pushed, scraped, and piled armfuls of snow up against the metal surrounding the fire, but it was like trying to blow out a highway flare. Only the thinness of the air at six thousand feet was retarding the combustion process. The drone of the fighters overhead was comforting. The crack and whine of the ricocheting bullets was not. Hudner wondered how long the fighter cover would be able to persuade the enemy to remain on the mountain slopes.

Looking up at Jesse, Hudner judged the cockpit to be at least seven or eight feet above the ground. He could get up there only by pulling himself up on the ice-covered, gull-shaped wings by grasping the edge of the cockpit and climbing from there onto the top of the fuselage.

By sitting astride the fuselage, he could talk to Jesse but accomplish little else. Another alternative was to stand on the tiny little step located on the left side of the fuselage just below the cockpit. The problem there was that it took both hands just to hold on.

"Jesse, I can't seem to maintain my balance well enough and still get any leverage."

"Yeah, I know. What we need is a crane."

His composure is really remarkable, Hudner thought, and he wondered how he would react if he were the one trapped inside the cockpit instead of Jesse. The bitter cold brought another thought to his mind.

"Here, take this. Maybe it'll help a little." So saying, he removed his white silk scarf and wrapped it around Jesse's bare hands. Noticing how stiff Jesse's fingers were, Hudner then produced a woolen navy-issue watch cap from a pocket in his flight suit and pulled it down over Jesse's unprotected head; he had pulled off his helmet when he landed.

"It isn't much, I know," said Hudner. Jesse's expression showed his thanks.

"I'm going over and see if my radio still works. Maybe I can raise Cevoli and find out if there is a helicopter coming."

As Hudner retraced his steps through the snow to his aircraft, he couldn't help wondering how the day would end. He was a long way from Fall River, Massachusetts, where he had grown up. His three brothers, his sister, and his parents had been extremely proud of his winning an appointment to the Naval Academy at Annapolis.

He had graduated as an ensign in 1946, a year after World War II ended. A tour on the heavy cruiser *Helena* had convinced him that he belonged in aviation.

He had received his wings at Pensacola in 1949 and was then transferred to NAS Quonset Point, Rhode Island, where he joined his first fighter squadron, VF-32, attached to the carrier *Leyte*. It was also here that he had met Jesse Brown. He had become friends with Jesse, but no more so than anyone else. Because it was a closely knit squadron, everyone got along well together, and Jesse was just one of the guys. His uniqueness was in being Black. He had asked for no special privileges and was accorded none. He was just another pilot. Hudner remembered that Jesse was serious-minded, like himself, but that his sense of humor invariably attracted people to him. Even though he was a junior officer, Jesse was well on his way to becoming a leader. He was on his way up.

As he reached his aircraft, Hudner was jolted out of his reverie by the pungent smell of aviation gasoline. To operate the radio, he must get back into the cockpit to turn on the battery. If there were any electrical shorts, one spark could blow everything sky high. *It's a risk I'll have to take,* decided Hudner. Gingerly, he seated himself in the cockpit, plugged in the radio cord, and flicked on the switch that read BATT. A slight click was the only result. Next, he flipped on a switch marked MASTER RADIO and waited for it to warm up.

"Able Leader, this is Able Four; this is Able Four. Do you read me? Over."

"Roger, Able Four, I read you, very weak, but readable. What's the situation down there?"

Hudner felt a surge of relief as he briefed Cevoli on their predicament.

"I need help. I need a fire extinguisher and an axe; better, I need a cutting torch. We've got to cut into the side of the fuselage. Jesse is pinned in the cockpit by the buckling of the fuselage. What about the chopper?"

"Roger, Able Four. I can barely hear you. A chopper is on the way. I just had contact with him. He's alone but says he has an axe and a fire extinguisher on board. He's about five minutes out. We're going to have to shove off now, Tom, due to our fuel state. Over."

Hudner's reply to Cevoli was never acknowledged. "Guess my battery has had it," he figured. "At least I got through." He secured the switches and climbed out of the cockpit. He trudged back and with great difficulty hauled himself up again to straddle the cockpit of Jesse's aircraft.

CHARLIE WARD in his Ho3S helicopter had already been briefed by Cevoli. He was startled to learn that now there were two people to rescue instead of one. He thought to himself that they had better not weigh much.

"This is Able Leader to rescue helicopter. Suggest you come in from the east if possible. Our fighter cover has reported heavy small-arms fire on the other three sides. It's accurate and intense," Cevoli offered. "We're low on fuel and will have to depart soon. Good luck!"

"Thanks, Able Leader. I'm coming in for a look-see." On his preliminary fly-by Charlie could see one pilot seated astride the smoking aircraft, apparently talking to the pilot in the cockpit. Now, as he made his final approach, Hudner was holding up an emergency smoke flare indicating the wind direction and strength. Charlie carefully set the helicopter down between the two crashed Corsairs and got out, leaving the engine idling.

"Hi," was his epic greeting.

"Do you have a fire extinguisher?" Hudner immediately asked.

"Yes, but it's pretty small."

"Well, you'd better get it. Apparently, the metal has caught fire and snow doesn't seem to have any effect on putting it out."

"OK, I've got a small axe, too, if that'll help. I heard you asked for one."

"Good, bring it, too."

Charlie made his way back to the helicopter. *If this engine should die,* he thought as he gathered up the axe and the extinguisher, *we'll all vacation here for the winter.* He noticed on the way back that even the slightest exertion required great effort.

Both Hudner and Charlie had recognized each other, although neither had acknowledged the fact. Ironically, it had been the carrier *Leyte* that had ferried the ten helicopters and Marine pilots overseas from Norfolk to Japan.

Charlie was equally surprised to see Jesse. He had been aware that he was the first and, at that time, the only Black aviator in the navy. He had spoken to him once or twice aboard ship and remembered Jesse as something of a celebrity. He had been practically worshiped by the other Black men on the ship. In fact, the fantail was always a very crowded place whenever Jesse was among the pilots returning from a mission to make his carrier landings. He was easily the most bragged-about pilot aboard, and his airmanship was a constant subject for discussion in the galley, where the majority of the ship's Black men were assigned. Charlie wondered what imponderable quirk of fate had singled out Jesse, from all three of the *Leyte*'s fighter squadrons, to be shot down.

Upon reaching the downed aircraft, Charlie handed the fire extinguisher to Hudner, who promptly sprayed the small stream toward the source of smoke in the accessory section. The smoke abated somewhat for a few moments, but then it poured out again. The fire was still burning.

"Foam is the only way to smother burning magnesium," Hudner commented.

Charlie nodded in agreement and glanced up toward the cockpit.

"Is he in pain?"

"Yes, I think so. He's really wedged in there. The problem is that you can't get any leverage against the fuselage to pull him out, not to mention trying to get any decent footing. That fuselage is impossible to work on without a ladder or without some way to stand right next to the cockpit."

Charlie was not yet convinced. "Well, let's both try and see what we can do. Seems like between us we ought to be able to pull him out."

Sitting astride the top of the fuselage, one in front and the other in back of Jesse, the two pilots each took one of his arms and heaved.

"No! No! Stop!" Jesse groaned in pain. "That's not going

to do it!" The look on his face told them they would have to find another way.

Back down on the ground, the two men stood in silence, each trying to think of some way to release their fellow pilot. Hudner picked up the small hand axe and went over to the right side of the aircraft. He swung mightily at the side of the fuselage several times with all the force he could muster.

"You might as well use your fists," Charlie said. "They built these things out of railroad tracks and boiler plate."

Unfortunately, Charlie was reasonably correct. The tiny nicks in the side of the Corsair were exactly proportionate to those on the now-dulled axe blade. Hudner's heavy breathing was the only sound that could be heard except that from the aircraft circling above.

A terrible fact was surfacing: It was apparent to both pilots that Jesse's tightly pinned leg was, by its presence, on the verge of entombing him.

The helicopter pilot said it first: "That leg has got to come off if we're ever going to get him out of there."

"I know," Hudner said, "but how? You'd have to stand on your head right on top of him and reach down in the cockpit to do it. Besides, all I've got is this survival knife." Hudner's words were all too true. In order to cut off a leg, you must first be able to reach it.

"I don't know if we could just cut the leg off," Charlie continued. "We would need a chopping action for the bone." Charlie's comment was again correct, and Hudner nodded his head in agreement.

Hudner carefully remounted the icy wing and stretched a snow-covered boot over to the narrow step just below the cockpit.

"How you doin', Jesse?" Hudner tried to sound encouraging.

Jesse looked at Hudner for a long moment but did not speak.

With an attempt at reassurance, Hudner continued, "We're going to try to figure out a way to get better leverage so we can loosen your leg a little."

Hudner slid down off the twisted fuselage, and the two pilots walked a short distance away to hold the ultimate conference. The results of this conference would determine the fate of each man involved.

Ward and Hudner left Jesse alone with his thoughts, for which there is no record. He had a wife named Daisy and a one-year-old daughter named Pamela, who had taken her first steps just days before his carrier had left for Korea. Jesse had hardly had time to become acquainted with her. He had his parents to wonder about—how they would take the news about him if it should turn out to be bad.

Injured and chilled, he must have wanted desperately to move around a little more, to get his blood moving better. If the sight of his airplane on fire, possibly with flames only a few short feet away, had alarmed him at first, by now he may have wished the flames were a little closer. (Whoever said freezing to death is painless obviously has never been there.)

If Jesse thought back over the events of the past few years, he could be satisfied that he had been not just unique but exemplary. He had broken a long-standing navy tradition preventing Blacks from being commissioned as aviators (the air force, incidentally, had no such tradition; one of his uncles had flown P-38s in World War II). There had never been a navy regulation prohibiting it; it just wasn't done. He had decided to apply anyway and was accepted. He had graduated about the middle of his aviation class of midshipmen at Pensacola. After completing the required probationary period, he had received his ensign's commission while at sea from Capt. W. L. Erdmann, the commanding officer of the aircraft carrier *Leyte*.

Jesse could have prided himself on fulfilling a difficult assignment as the first in a challenging role. He must have known that he was generally well liked, just as he was aware that a few were predisposed to tolerate him. His friends could vouch for how carefully he chose his friends, always aware of others' unexpressed beliefs or prejudices. He had to have known, sitting there trapped in a smoking Corsair, that he had tried to avoid being controversial and instead had concentrated on doing his job well. Raised by deeply religious parents, he would have had a faith to turn to; he had assisted at services in the small chapel at NAS Quonset Point, Rhode Island, and also in the Protestant services aboard the carrier.

The sound of rounds striking the ground near the Corsair interrupted his reminiscence and brought his attention back to the desperate present. He probably knew the right leg was as good as gone, but his left leg, the good one, was numb, too. The thought of losing a leg by now may not have seemed so bad. Everybody knew about one-legged pilots who were still flying. But he also would have known, from his first-aid training, that if they were able to cut the right leg off, he would bleed to death within ten or twenty minutes without a proper tourniquet. He had no idea how long the helicopter would take to get him to medical aid. Jesse probably did not know that, in any event, the helicopter could not lift three people, perhaps not even two.

Th Hudner-Ward conference was drawing to a close. It was now 4:50 p.m., and complete darkness was not far away. Jesse had been sitting in his deep freeze for more than an hour and a half.

"I guess you're right," Charlie was saying. "I don't see any way of amputating that leg. If we could just swing the axe, I think we could do it and then get him out of the cockpit. We're only about twenty-five minutes from Hagaru; there's a doctor there." Hudner did not reply.

"Yes," Charlie went on, "it looks like the only way is to cut the side of the fuselage away and try to free the leg."

Hudner, still quiet, pondered what he had just heard and waited for Charlie to continue. Perhaps he expected the older man intuitively to know a way.

"It would take a month to hack through that metal with just a hand axe," Charlie grimaced, as he thought out loud, presenting the pros and cons of each idea.

"Well, what's the alternative?" Hudner finally asked. "We can't pull him out, and we can't get to his right leg well enough to cut it off. He's obviously got to be freed from the outside. We'd need some kind of cutting torch for that."

Charlie looked long and thoughtfully at his flying boots before replying.

"Yes, you're right."

The next question was unnecessary. Both pilots were aware that the nearest cutting torch would be back at the airfield at Hungnam, if they had one at all, and that was more than fifty miles in each direction.

Both men became aware of the sudden quiet that had descended on them, as the fighters above had finally been forced to leave because of darkness. With great reluctance, Cevoli and Koenig had departed toward their rendezvous with a pitching flight deck and a night carrier landing. Their fuel was dangerously low, and they had done all they could do. Cevoli had already released the other fighters to preclude any further mishaps. If he and Koenig ran out of fuel in their landing approach, the freezing water would claim them as casualties. But however poor their chances, he knew he and

Koenig were better off than those guys down there in the snow.

"It's GETTING dark now, almost too dark to see the hills," Charlie broke the silence. "We've got to make a move."

Hudner did not respond. He had come too far in his personal war with the elements and felt too totally frustrated and helpless to be able to say anything. It was too difficult to accept the fact that he and Charlie had reached the end of the road, and they were not going to be able to free Jesse from the broken Corsair. They both had worked and sweated and fought for more than an hour and had been able to accomplish exactly nothing—except to be with Jesse.

"I'm afraid we're holding a losing hand, Tom. Are you going to tell him?" Charlie looked Hudner directly into his eyes.

Hudner slowly nodded, took a deep resolute breath, and headed back toward Jesse's aircraft. He climbed once again onto the ice-covered wing and stretched his right leg over to the tiny step.

"Jesse, there isn't any way we can do it. We can't get enough leverage to pull you out, and we haven't got anything that'll even dent this iron bird. We can't even get into your cockpit to amputate the leg. We can't get you out."

Jesse's composure would become a part of Hudner's life, too. The two men stared at each other briefly, and then Jesse broke the silence.

"I understand. I appreciate what you both have done. I've already accepted the fact. It won't prove a thing for you guys to stand around here and freeze to death."

He paused for a moment, knowing he was speaking the last few words that anyone would hear. "Please tell Daisy how much I love her and that she's in my thoughts right now."

"I will, Jesse. Do you want another morphine Syrette?"

"No, just go. Good luck, Hud. I hope you make it."

Hudner got down off the step and joined Charlie, who was standing a few feet away. The two pilots walked over and climbed into the still-idling helicopter. Charlie brought the engine up to speed and engaged the rotor blades. The helicopter skidded forward through the snow, over the icy surface, and staggered into the air. Twenty minutes later they landed at Hagaru-ri in a circle of headlights provided by jeeps. Neither pilot had spoken during the ride back.

And so, in a cold forgotten valley in North Korea, the first Black naval aviator died. He died bravely and alone, leaving behind a legacy of inspiration for every man and woman who must at some time put his or her life on the line.

It is only for God to know whether the fire, the cold, or the enemy stilled Jesse Brown's heart forever.

EPILOGUE

Lt. (jg) Thomas Hudner, USN, "for conspicuous gallantry and intrepidity at the risk of his life above and beyond the call of duty as a pilot," was awarded the Congressional Medal of Honor by President Truman in April 1951. He was one of only two naval aviators to receive the nation's highest award in the Korean War for performance of duty during flying operations.

For his efforts to rescue Ens. Jesse Brown and Lieutenant (jg) Hudner, Capt. Charles C. Ward received the Silver Star, the nation's third highest award, "for extraordinary bravery."

In 1972 the United States Navy commissioned a destroyer escort (DE-1089) memorializing Ens. Jesse L. Brown, only the third Black man ever to have had a naval vessel named in his honor.

4

A One-Eyed Miracle
at Guadalcanal

When old pilots sit around in their living rooms and home-built wet bars, reliving and retelling war stories, invariably someone says, "Boy, I remember my first solo flight at Pensacola," or "That first carrier night cat-shot was awesome," and so on into the night. Most aviators remember their first combat mission as well. The majority of such first missions are usually ordinary, even routine. Experienced flight leaders want their very new and green pilots to check out the area, to get a handle on things before charging off to do battle with the enemy.

In Ken Reusser's case the circumstances at his South Pacific base did not lend themselves to the luxuries of area familiarization flights, much less to get-acquainted-with-your-airplane hops. In other words, "Pilots, man your planes. This is war, second lieutenants included."

As first combat missions go, Reusser's would be very hard to top—even from the security of that comfortable armchair.

EPTEMBER AND October, 1942, spanned a period of frantic warfare as the Japanese intensified their efforts to reinforce Guadalcanal. U.S. forces were still on the defensive on many fronts in the South Pacific. Marine squadrons VMF-212, -223, -224, VMO-251, and others had been waging a war of attrition on land, at sea, and in the air for several months. VMF-121 (of Joe Foss fame) arrived at the scene in September. VMF-122, once brought up to strength, was to be fully activated sometime in November.

On 14 October, Second Lieutenant Reusser was a recently arrived, newly trained "nugget" who had just completed his transitional F4F training at Camp Kearney, San Diego (now NAS Miramar). Ken had accumulated all of thirty-nine hours in the Grumman Wildcat. His squadron, VMF-122, was in an indoctrination and checkout status and was scheduled to begin flying in a few days. Their newly completed airstrip was on Espíritu Santo in the Santa Cruz Island chain and was located about 550 miles southeast of Guadalcanal.

The operational plan was to feed in replacement pilots from Espíritu Santo to Marine Air Groups 14 and 23, whose pilots were flying daily sorties from Henderson Field in the Solomons.

The next day, October 15, a priority air-search mission for some downed American pilots in the greater Guadalcanal area was scheduled. Ken's first mission in a combat area was at hand. There would be no time for a fam hop, an area checkout, or a flight to get reacquainted with the aircraft. It was a launch! The pilots' .38 caliber revolvers had not even been issued yet. In fact, Ken and several other young officers (Milt Cook, Sam Richards, Ron Meyers, and Hal Roach) had nefariously acquired over two thousand rounds of .30 caliber ammo back at Noumea, where five days earlier they had disembarked from the SS *Lurline*. The converted luxury liner had provided the marines a luxury cruise, if you overlooked the six-men-to-a-room accommodations. The lieutenants had also stumbled upon some fully automatic army Reising machine guns, with which they had proceeded to terrorize the Noumean neighborhood with their version of weapons-familiarization exercises. These machine guns, complete with metal folding stocks, were still in their possession at Espíritu Santo.

"Just the perfect cockpit sidearm for a fighter pilot," Milt Cook had remarked, sardonically.

A flight of 12 F4F-4s was scheduled to take off at 1300 to fly in three four-plane divisions in a line-abreast formation so as to cover as wide a search pattern as possible. The assigned search altitude was a thousand feet.

Capt. Nate Post was the flight leader and 1st Lt. Hal Roach, later killed on Guadalcanal, was assigned as Ken's division leader. The search sector was in the quadrant southwest of the Solomon Islands.

The mission was to be of maximum duration, with a final landing anticipated either at or just after sunset. With drop tanks, the maximum time aloft for the F4F-4 was around six hours. The large number of downed U.S. pilots had over-whelmed the limited rescue capabilities of the navy's PBY Catalina fleet. Radio silence was to be observed, and no enemy aircraft encounters were anticipated, particularly at the search altitude of only a thousand feet. Running lights were to be utilized to better maintain visual contact within the widely spaced formation. By chance, Ken's position in the flight was at the extreme outer left side.

The takeoff and rendezvous for all twelve Wildcats went as briefed. *What a first flight,* Ken thought. *I'm out here at the edge of nothing. I hope Captain Post got good marks at Pensacola.*

Every cloud shadow and whitecap appeared, momentarily, to be a possible life raft, and time dragged for Ken with nothing but silence on the radio. After about three hours into the flight, a speck appeared in Ken's windscreen at ten o'clock, very low on the water.

No doubt one of ours, figured Ken, *coming back to Espíritu from his search mission.* The speck grew larger, and, just at his abeam position, a "meatball" marking the aircraft as enemy became quite distinguishable. Battle stations! It was a Japanese Betty bomber for sure. Ken pressed the mike button: "Japanese bomber, nine o'clock, right on the deck, opposite heading."

He waited a few seconds for an acknowledgment from the flight leader, knowing that the enemy aircraft would disappear in just moments. Decision time!

Ken would later call this a "second-lieutenant decision." He commenced a hard diving turn and, with an adrenaline assist, shoved the throttle and RPM to full power. As he charged all six 50-caliber machine guns, he called again on the radio.

"This is Bravo 12, I say again, have Japanese bomber in sight, course 160 degrees. Am closing. Request acknowledge, Bravo Leader. Please acknowledge, over."

The response was still dead silence. Though his closure rate was agonizingly slow, he was sure his top speed would allow him to overtake the Betty. He could not remember what the Betty's top speed was or, for that matter, his own. His only thought was to shoot down the enemy.

Finally, as the distance decreased from the enemy's seven o'clock position to firing range, he pressed the trigger. The noise of all six .50-caliber machine guns filled the cockpit as his tracers arced slowly beneath the bomber. He was still out of range. All he had done was to alert the Japanese gunners

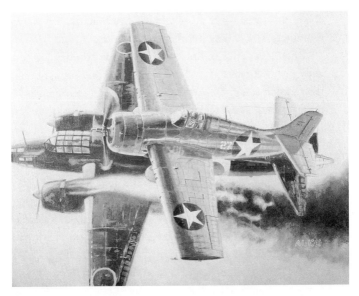

Lt. Ken Reusser shoots down a Japanese Betty bomber on his first combat mission. *painting by Alex Durr*

of his presence. He could see the winking of the bomber's left dorsal machine gun where the enemy's rounds, like his, were falling even shorter. Ken banked left and right instinctively to throw off the opposing gunners' aim. Ken guessed he was only about fifty feet above the water, too low to dive under the Betty and fire from underneath. He suddenly remembered from his aircraft recognition lectures that the bomber had a 20-mm cannon in the tail turret, which fortunately was strangely quiet.

As the bomber filled the gunsight, Ken squeezed the trigger again. Immediately the Japanese aircraft's port engine caught fire. The bomber slowed, skidded to the left, pulled up sharply, and then cartwheeled into the sea. As Ken climbed above the scene, only an oily black swath across the water remained. The enemy bomber was no more.

"Bravo Leader from Bravo 12. Splash one bomber. Do you copy, over?" Again silence. Several repeated calls brought only the familiar quiet. *Surely they must have heard me. Someone in the flight must have.* Breaking radio silence to report an enemy sighting was OK, Ken knew. It was SOP.

My radio must be the culprit, Ken surmised, as he climbed back to altitude in preparation for the long flight home on a course he hoped would take him to Espíritu Santo.

Suddenly it dawned on him. In the excitement of sighting the Betty, he had committed an absolute no-no. Naval aviators do not break formation and go tearing off on their own, even to shoot down an enemy aircraft. Their briefing, if you could call it that, had not addressed the subject of enemy aircraft encounters. It had been a casual, "Let's go look for our downed buddies, and we'll see you all back at home base, etc." sort of thing. There had been no official support for his decision to go after the enemy aircraft, either, but he could not have known that his radio was out while observing radio silence. Besides, his decision had been made in a heartbeat. He would address this problem later, as the challenge of finding his way home was of a more pressing nature.

A macabre thought crossed his mind. If he didn't make it back, they couldn't very well line up a firing squad or even make him permanent squadron duty officer.

After almost two hours of searching for land of any kind and numerous fruitless calls, Ken became aware of several facts: He was lost, not just *maybe* lost. He was down to about ten to fifteen minutes of fuel. He had to land or ditch while some daylight remained, and if he had to ditch, it was safer to do so with power.

A few minutes after sunset, a concerned and resigned F4F

pilot jettisoned his belly tank, opened and locked the canopy, put down his flaps and tail hook, turned into the wind, and said a quick prayer out loud. The latter turned out to be his most important action.

The Wildcat skipped lightly across the wave tops, almost daintily, and then smashed into a huge solid swell. Because he had no shoulder straps (they were not yet in use in the Wildcat), the momentum of the sudden stop slammed Ken's head into the gun sight. The canopy also slammed forward to the closed position, easily overpowering the tiny locking device.

Upon regaining consciousness, Ken could sense that he was under water and that the aircraft was sinking. He released his safety belt and, bending over, somehow forced the canopy loose from its rails. Taking a deep breath, he began to swim toward the light that signaled the surface.

Almost immediately he realized that the light was becoming dimmer, and his eardrums told him he was still sinking. Groping wildly, he found that his parachute had spilled during the crash and the shroud lines were taking him to a watery grave. Grasping the saw-toothed survival knife that he had brought along from the States, he hacked with all his might at the nylon parachute lines to free himself. Then he lost consciousness again. Moments later he bobbed to the surface and gulped in fresh air in huge quantities. Amazingly, he had managed to pull one of the two toggles of his Mae West.

After gathering his senses, Ken began taking a personal inventory as he floated in the warm tropical water. The left side of his face was numb and bleeding profusely. His life raft had gone down with the plane, as had his life-saving survival knife, along with that wonderful folding machine gun, which he had carefully stowed in the cockpit for a rainy day.

The bleeding soon attracted sharks, which began circling

him. They were curious but did not attack him. Desiring to diminish the reason for their attention, he found that he could slow the bleeding by pressing his left arm tightly against his head. He had swallowed both salt water and his own blood, which had promptly been thrown up. The pain was bearable, probably because everything was still pretty numb. Ken noticed that he could see out of only his right eye.

It was now quite dark, and the battered aviator accepted the fact that he might not survive. As the hours passed, he drifted off into numb semiconsciousness. Though he could no longer see the sharks, he somehow sensed that they had departed. (For reasons never understood, the sharks had indeed left. Perhaps, as Ken later said, they didn't like his blood type.)

Shortly after midnight, having spent almost seven hours in the water, Ken heard what sounded like a repeated "Wahoo" cry. Since any cry was welcome, even a Japanese one, he located his whistle and blew it. After several shouts and whistles, he was pulled into a small dugout canoe by three large and very strong natives. After being handed a bottle of something, Ken drank heavily and gratefully. His rescuers then gently laid him down in the canoe on some coconut mats. The beverage was not the expected water but rather a harsh, vile-tasting, burning liquid. Though unappealing, it stayed down, and so did he. Whatever the concoction was, it put him to sleep immediately.

Sometime later, Ken awoke to find himself being lifted from the canoe by some willing arms as daylight approached. He could feel gentle hands as they undressed him and carefully washed away the dried blood on his neck and face. He felt a gauze compress being placed against the battered left side of his head and then gauze being wrapped around and around, like a turban. Soon he again dropped into a deep sleep, not awakening until the next night. The gauze bandages, he learned later, had been left by some missionaries who had lived for a short while among the natives before fleeing when the Japanese arrived.

Though communication was difficult, it was immediately apparent that the natives were friendly to downed American pilots and that they, too, hated and feared the Japanese. Through pidgin English and a lot of "pointee-talkee," Ken also learned that they would hide, feed, and care for him. He thought that perhaps they would somehow get help, too, but this was not clearly understood.

The natives, of course curious but also anxious to help, had established an efficient organization that reminded Ken of the navy's system aboard ship. One group of women acted as the mess cooks, preparing the food and feeding him. Another female group formed the medical department and took turns, twenty-four hours a day, dripping warm salt water from a coconut shell directly onto the compress bandage. The seawater was continually warmed over some low coals in an adjoining hut. Ken decided they somehow knew it was important to keep the bandage moist and the eye covered. They would not allow him to remove the compress, even to examine the wound. They kept him unaware of what they had seen: his left eye dangling from its socket.

Another group of natives, this one consisting of men, acted as the security department. When calls of nature were required, they would escort Ken to the designated officer's bush, constantly placing their fingers to their lips to indicate silence and warn that the Japanese were not far away.

Ken's meals were not fancy but, as he commented later, "The service was first class." The menu consisted primarily of coconut meat, coconut milk, papaya, sweet potatoes, and once an "almost" chicken stew. He was sure they had sacrificed their only chicken for him. Since it lasted for several days, the natives had apparently saved it all for him.

The personal sanitation department was the most unusual one. Even though they themselves knew it was entirely unnecessary, the natives had evidently learned from the missionaries that all white people needed to bathe daily. Consequently, each day just at sundown the security department would dutifully escort Ken to an open air "bathing spot," which, oddly enough, was in the center of the small village. All hands assembled, as if for the evening movie aboard ship, to watch with rapt attention as the same women of the medical section carefully washed the white body of the stark naked and embarrassed marine pilot. The tepid salt water did little to preserve the dignity of the fallen warrior.

After the bathing ceremony concluded, each villager would walk by and touch Ken's arm or shoulder in an almost reverent manner. This simple and friendly gesture was usually accompanied by a stained or toothless grin.

Keeping track of time was a real problem, since Ken's watch was lost when he ditched. He solved this dilemma by putting cats-eye seashells in half of a coconut shell, one for each day. (He learned that these seashells were also used for jewelry and bartering.) The natives were impressed by his method of keeping track of the days, perhaps because there was, in their view, no need to keep track of time. Tomorrow always came, seashells or not.

On the morning of the fourteenth seashell, the transportation department showed up. They were the same three natives who had found him floating in his Mae West two weeks earlier. The village chief, who was also one of the dugout rescuers, proceeded to inform Ken that help was on the way. A great bird would fly into their lagoon to take him far away to another land, he announced. This would happen when the sun reached the water's edge. The boatmen would take him out into the lagoon where the great bird would be waiting. A great warrior on another island had spoken with Ken's friends. (This great warrior turned out to be a gallant Australian coast watcher who had radioed the U.S. Navy about the downed airman.)

As announced, just at dusk a large American patrol plane approached the island, very low on the water. Before boarding the canoe, Ken bade a tearful one-eyed goodbye to the villagers, paying particular attention to the ladies of the medical section. He would always wonder how they had learned that the continuous application of warm salt water would halt or minimize the infection process.

This time the canoe paddlers offered no beverage service. Soon a navy PBY landed alongside the dugout, and the three natives helped him up and into the Catalina's starboard blister. There was no fighter escort, but the takeoff and departure went smoothly, with no interference from the Japanese. Ken figured that they must have heard and seen the PBY land and take off but could not react quickly enough to thwart their escape. It was never known whether the Japanese took any retaliatory measures against the natives.

The three-hour return flight to Espíritu Santo gave the corpsman aboard the Catalina the opportunity to examine the head wound. The PBY crew had not been informed that their rescuee had been injured, and the corpsman turned a pale green when he removed the soggy compresses. All he could do was replace the bandages with clean ones. He then told Ken that there was some infection and, for the first time, the flier learned that his eye was actually out of its socket.

When Ken arrived aboard the seaplane tender USS *Kitty Hawk* (AVP-1), a navy flight surgeon worked on him diligently. The orbital socket was badly broken, and a skin flap had

Friendly natives paddle Lieutenant Reusser to a waiting Navy PBY for his return flight to Espíritu Santo. *painting by Alex Durr*

already started to grow over the empty socket. After first treating the infection for two days, the doctor was able to re-implant the eyeball and suture shut the surrounding skin. The result was an ugly, red, painful-looking welt. Although Ken could see reasonably well, the doctor would make no commitment as to future vision in that eye. Fortunately, the eye and the socket did heal, with the vision from his left eye only partially restricted by the skin flap still attached above his cheek. The native women had done their work wonderfully well.

After three weeks, Ken returned to flight status, by virtue of just showing up at Airfield Operations. He discovered then that his squadron had since departed for Guadalcanal, he had been declared missing in action, and his next of kin had been notified. There had been an aerial search for him the two days following his ditching, but with the vast expanse of ocean to be covered, not to mention an intense battle being fought in the Solomons, Ken had been considered a regrettable casualty. The airmen his squadron had been sent to find were never sighted.

Interestingly, officials conducted no formal board of inquiry, nor did Ken make an accident report. Since there was a war on, his only claims to fame were his big ugly welt and the fact that he was back, ready for action.

However, his conscience was not as clear as his vision. Upon considering the matter during the fourteen days with the natives and almost three weeks of recuperation, he decided not to claim the Japanese bomber, concluding that his immature rush to combat more than canceled out his aerial victory. Even though no living person knew he had left the formation without permission, he knew. In his mind, he had made an error of judgment that the downed enemy bomber could not offset. He carried this incident with him secretly for fifty-four years.

Ken conducted ferry flights between Espíritu Santo to Guadalcanal for three more months until a marine general saw him and ordered him home for reconstructive surgery. He returned to the States in February 1943, reporting to the U.S. Naval Hospital in San Diego, California, for further medical treatment.

EPILOGUE

Kenneth L. Reusser went on to achieve the rank of colonel. He flew 213 combat missions in World War II, Korea, and Vietnam and eventually received forty-nine decorations and awards. These include two Navy Crosses, Legion of Merit with Combat "V," five Distinguished Flying Crosses, and four Purple Hearts. He retired in 1968 and lives with his wife, Trudy, in Beaverton, Oregon. Ironically, after all the reconstructive surgeries, his damaged left eye today is his "good" eye.

5 A One-Armed Carrier Landing

THE ODDS ON flying a Roger pass, getting a cut from the landing signal officer and catching an early wire in an F4U-4 Corsair on a narrow, straight-deck CVL are fairly reasonable, with everything going for you. Throw in a pitching flight deck surrounded by 32-degree water, and the old pucker factor rises. But for a pilot flying with only one usable arm, the odds on that Roger pass decrease dramatically.

Such was the case for marine captain Albert Grasselli flying off the USS *Bataan* (CVL-29) with VMF-212 just off the west coast of Korea near Inchon. The date was January 20, 1951, during the coldest winter ever recorded in North Korea.

The division of four Corsairs had been catapulted several hours earlier from the flight deck of *Bataan*. Their mission was an armed reconnaissance flight to search and destroy a reported truck column near Haiju, North Korea.

Capt. Grasselli was Fox Flight Division Leader. Flying his wing was Capt. Al Agan, with the squadron only three days but a combat veteran of World War II. Leading the second

Replacement pilots at Itazuke Air Force Base in Japan, en route to join their squadron aboard the USS *Bataan*. *Left to right:* Capt. Al Agan, 1st Lt. Don Tooker, an unidentified Air Force pilot, Lt. Col. Tom Ahern, and 1st Lt. Norm Turley. This was the last photograph ever taken of Agan.

section was 1st Lt. Charlie Rice, and on his wing was 1st Lt. Bill Siegfried.

The flight had progressed smoothly, although they had not located the reported truck column. Instead, from information passed to them from another flight, they had diverted from their assigned mission to bomb and strafe some reported troop emplacements about twenty miles north of Haiju. Light antiaircraft fire had been reported by the other flight.

"Fox Leader, this is Easy One. We didn't take any hits but they've got small arms and possibly some bigger stuff higher up on the hills to the east. Recommend you pull out left toward the sea."

"Roger. Thanks, Easy Leader. We're about ten miles south of the Haiju power plant chimney, headed your position. Is that black smoke under you now?"

"That's affirm, Fox One. We're leaving the area but we'll remain on this frequency until feet wet."

"OK, Easy One . . . break, break. Fox One to flight. Go column and check all switches hot, but charge guns only on run-in. We'll drop 500-pounders on the first run and strafe on the second. All pullouts left. Repeat, only two runs."

A "Roger" from each pilot assured Grasselli that the flight understood his instructions. "We'll roll in at ten thousand feet and pull out no lower than two thousand. Be alert for any AA."

The flight wheeled gracefully under the clear skies in a smooth arc and one by one followed Fox One into their runs. No one spoke as each pilot concentrated on the target and pipper sight alignment.

"Fox One, clear."

"Fox Two, clear."

"Fox Three, clear."

"Fox Four, clear. No AA observed."

"Roger from Fox One. We'll level off at three thousand for our strafing runs."

"Fox One from Two. I think I've got a problem. I ran into something on the pullout."

"Affirmative. Looks like he's trailing smoke or hydraulic fluid. I'm closing now," from the Number Three man.

"Fox Two from One. How are your instruments?"

"Aah . . . Roger. They seem to read OK. Oil pressure is a tad low but the temp is right."

"Fox Leader from Three. He's trailing oil from the right oil cooler. Hard to say how much but it looks to be considerable."

"Roger, Three. Fox Two, shut off your right oil cooler bypass. Fox Flight, we'll head for the coast. Fox Three, stay tight on him."

Images of a water landing versus an emergency landing in enemy-held territory entered each pilot's mind. Captain Agan was in serious trouble, with possibly only a few precious minutes of powered flight remaining.

"Fox One, this is Payette [Capt. Jim Payette of VMF-212] in Easy One. Understand you've got an emergency. Remember Cho-Do-Ri, the island just off the coast, is friendly—if he can make it that far. We'll cover you but only for a little bit. We're almost at bingo fuel."

"Thanks, Jim. Fox Two, what state?"

Agan in Fox Two had already made a right turn heading out across Inchon Inlet on a direct course for Cho-Do-Ri, as he'd heard the other flight leader's comments regarding the friendly island. Several minutes passed in silence, as if each pilot were holding his breath.

"This is Fox Two. Oil pressure is falling pretty steadily. Temp is coming up, too. Don't know if I can make it to that island."

"Roger, Fox Two." By now they were just halfway across Inchon Inlet. Grasselli was reluctant to give orders to Fox Two, as is often the case. The pilot of a single-seat aircraft has to make the final decision, based on the situation and his own judgment, in an actual emergency.

"This is Fox Two. The cylinder head temp just pegged." Again, no one spoke. It was decision time.

"This is Fox Two. I'm going to have to ditch now. The prop just froze. Save my seat in the wardroom."

"Roger, Fox Two. We'll cover you. Fox Three and Four, get some altitude and get out a Mayday. Request the ship's rescue chopper ASAP. I'll stay low with Fox Two."

Captain Agan's Corsair was descending rapidly toward the icy water below.

"Lock your canopy open, Al, and check shoulder straps.

The rescue H03-S Sikorsky helicopter attached to the *Bataan*. The pilot and crewman, shown here in their exposure suits, attempted to rescue Captain Agan. This is the same model of helicopter used by 1st Lt. Charlie Ward in chapter 3.

Suggest 15- to 20-degree flaps. Watch your airspeed and good luck! We've called for the chopper."

All radios were silent again as Agan skimmed the almost flat sea and prepared to ditch. The touchdown was abrupt, leaving only a short white mark on the water. In less than thirty seconds, the pilot exited the cockpit and a few minutes later the F4U raised its tail momentarily in a final salute and then slipped beneath the surface.

"Fox One from Three. The chopper is inbound at max speed. He was already airborne as plane guard. He estimates about twenty to twenty-five minutes."

"Roger, Fox Three. Thanks. Stay on station and help guide him in. Easy Flight has departed . . . I've got Fox Two in sight in the water, but he's not getting into his raft. Must be having trouble with it or maybe didn't have time to get it out of the cockpit. Even with the exposure suit, he doesn't have very long."

The remaining three Corsairs continued to orbit the crash scene, with Grasselli circling slowly just above the downed pilot. All of the pilots were wearing the navy's uncomfortable but required rubberized exposure suits. They made breathing difficult if the neck cinch was pulled up tightly, so they were usually worn somewhat loosely.

"This is Fox One, he's in his Mae West, but he's still not in his raft. I'm going to drop him mine."

So saying, Grasselli undid his safety belt and shoulder straps and, with Herculean effort, somehow managed to loosen and slide the one-man life raft out from the parachute beneath him.

With the raft removed, his already limited visibility from the cockpit was reduced even further; he was now sitting some ten inches lower in his seat.

Slowing down, he cranked open the canopy, extended full flaps, and dropped down to fifty feet. The numbing slipstream served to strengthen his resolve to get another life raft to his downed wingman.

Figuring the lead like a duck hunter, he tossed the raft out of the left side of the cockpit. Immediately, the entire left side of his upper body went numb. The slipstream had wrenched the raft from his grasp before he was ready to release it. Out of the corner of his eye he saw the raft splash down within a few feet of the pilot in the water.

"This is Fox Leader. Looks like I've got a small problem, too. I think my left shoulder is dislocated. Can't use it at all. Slipstream caught it."

After several moments of stunned silence: "Roger, Fox One from Three. What are your intentions?"

Once again the air remained quiet for almost a full minute. Grasselli was now in a predicament—not as serious as Fox

Two's, he realized, but flying a Corsair with two hands was always a demanding job. Just closing the canopy had been agonizingly difficult. He could still fly and manage the cockpit functions, but he certainly was no longer an effective rescue coordinator.

This problem was solved suddenly as a fresh flight of four squadron aircraft appeared on the scene to relieve Fox Flight on station and assume rescue coordination responsibility.

"Fox One from Three. We're approaching low fuel state. Suggest we join on you. The YE-ZB signal is Mike [carrier's navigation homer]. Course to the ship is 225 degrees."

Then it hit Grasselli. The ship! *My God, how am I going to get aboard with one arm?* He would need medical attention for sure, and very soon. The numbness had now turned to severe pain.

Granted, friendly airfields were perhaps too far away. But homing instincts are always strong in aviators' minds, particularly the minds of carrier pilots. He continued to weigh his alternatives. They would have a doctor right on the flight deck. The approach, the cut, the landing? Well, he'd give it his best shot.

"Roger, Fox Three, from One. Lead us back. I can't fly a very tight wing, though."

The three aircraft homed in on the beacon and entered the landing pattern as they received their "Signal Charlie," permission to land.

The LSO, Capt. Russell Patterson, had talked with Grasselli and knew that recovering a one-armed pilot aboard a carrier would be a challenge for all concerned.

"Al, this is Russ. Suggest we bring Fox Three and Four aboard first. Can you handle a wave-off if necessary?"

"Negative to that, Paddles. I'll follow Three and Four in.

Let's work for one good pass, but I'm afraid to try a wave-off unless it's way out in the groove. Once at the ramp, I've got to chop it."

"Roger from Paddles. Al, we'll have you in the ready room in a couple of minutes."

Well, at least he*'s got confidence,* Grasselli thought. He had managed to lower the gear, put down full flaps, open and lock the canopy, and finally lock the tail wheel, all with a great deal of pain.

The freezing slipstream this time had worked in his favor by clearing his head. *Ninety-five knots abeam of the island, right hand across to the throttle, back to the stick, back to the throttle, like a yo-yo. Prop and mixture full forward, 90 knots at the 90, check trim tabs*—this time reaching way across the cockpit and down low with the right hand. He could see Fox Three taxiing past the barriers and Fox Four coming out of the gear.

"Fox One, you're looking good. Keep it turning, don't get slow. You have a clear deck." Grasselli recognized the assistant LSO's voice and knew that both LSOs were doing their utmost to bring him safely aboard.

Eighty-five knots in the groove, still turning slightly at the ramp. Cut! Level the wings, right hand quickly to the throttle and immediately back to the stick for the nose-over and flare. A little late on the nose-over, he realized, as he sailed down the deck toward the barriers.

Engagement! Shoulder strap bites into the painful shoulder. *Mixture full aft, mags off.* Grasselli drifted into welcome unconsciousness as friendly hands lifted him gently out of the cockpit. He had caught the last wire. The flight deck officer had prudently lowered the two aft barriers.

The squadron flight surgeon, Lt. Cdr. Walter Jarvis, set Grasselli's dislocated shoulder, and he resumed flying duties less than a week later.

An F4U-4 Corsair lands on the deck of the *Bataan*. The very narrow flight deck made each landing a challenge.

Meanwhile, back in the Inchon Inlet, things were not as successful. The H03S-1 rescue helicopter had arrived in less than twenty-five minutes, and the downed pilot was easily spotted underneath the circling Corsairs. Captain Agan had not inflated the one-man life raft thrown to him by the flight leader. As the chopper came to a hover directly over the pilot in the water, the crew chief, wearing a special frogman cold-water suit, had jumped in the freezing water. After attaching the rescue sling around the pilot, both were hauled up into the passenger compartment. Captain Agan was dead from hypothermia.

The Sikorsky helicopter returned to the ship, where the squadron flight surgeon confirmed that the pilot had succumbed to the frigid waters.

EPILOGUE

I was a wingman in Easy Flight, Captain Payette's division, and then a first lieutenant. The sight of my good friend and roommate being lowered to the carrier's flight deck, frozen as stiff as a telephone pole, still remains graphically in my mind. I vividly remember thinking, at the time of his decision, *Al, don't try to make it out across the water to Cho-Do-Ri! Make a wheels-up landing on the mud flats right below. We've got enough friendly air support aircraft to hold off an enemy battalion.* But I didn't say a damn word. I just sat there figuring that Al would know best what to do. It was *his* emergency, not mine. But in my heart I was sure he would never make it to the friendly island some fifteen miles away. Captain Payette's well-meant suggestion was only that: an additional bit of information for Al to consider. Unfortunately, he took it as his only course of action. It cost him his life.

Nobody can go back and change things like this, but it still hurts to remember it . . . and always will. Everyone had done his best to save Capt. Al Agan, but the elements proved to be the superior force. Even Captain Grasselli's courageous actions were not enough to rescue his wingman.

Major Grasselli is retired and resides in McLean, Virginia. First Lt. Charlie Rice was killed in combat shortly after this incident; his wingman, Bill Siegfried, retired as a major and lives, at last report, in Tucson, Arizona.

6 Doing It the Hard Way

The setting is 1945, and it is still the same World War II for Ken Reusser, now a captain, serving his second tour overseas. Reusser hopes it will be less eventful than his first.

The Japanese are desperately trying to stave off an invasion of their mainland, although they know it is coming. They have resorted to mass suicide flights in a vain effort to sink U.S. warships. Their kamikaze tactics are becoming more effective because of the daring high-altitude photo reconnaissance they are conducting in specially modified two-engine aircraft. This "Nick" (the U.S. designation) takes pictures of the Pacific Fleet anchored off Okinawa early each morning. The photo plane then returns to Tokyo, where the films are developed. The awaiting kamikaze pilots, now armed with the exact locations of the American capital ships, take off on their one-way mission to death, both for them and for many American sailors.

The order of the day is: "Get that photo plane!" This is easier said than done, as it flies above the service ceiling of

> *all U.S. aircraft and also the protective ship-borne antiair-*
> *craft fire.*
>
> *Captain Reusser has an idea to counteract this high-*
> *altitude threat.*

IN THE EARLY morning darkness of 10 May 1945, four F4U-4
Corsairs rolled down the airstrip at Kadena, Okinawa, their
mission unique in the annals of World War II. Just off the
recently acquired island of Okinawa lay one of the world's
largest assemblies of fighting vessels, a U.S. armada consisting of every conceivable type of ship, from the largest carrier
and battleship to the smallest picket ship.

The Japanese were only too aware of the Americans' plan
to invade their empire in the very near future. They had
suffered extremely heavy losses at all fronts, but the decima-
tion of their aircraft and experienced flight crews had neces-
sitated a drastic change in their island defense strategy. The
ever-dwindling supply of aviation fuel and lubricants com-
pounded the problems facing the Japanese military planners.
Pilots with as little as thirty or forty hours were no match
for the well-trained American pilots. The appalling solution
to this problem, as the world would soon learn, was the
introduction of the "one-way ride to glory," with immediate
entrance into heaven: The kamikaze had arrived.

But in order to attack an American ship of significance,
the kamikaze pilot had to know where it was. To achieve this
knowledge, the Japanese turned to their twin-engine long-
range fighter, the Kawasaki Ki-45 Toryu Dragon Killer, called
"Nick" by Allied forces. The Nick was originally designed
in 1939 and remained in production until July 1945. Many
versions were manufactured. They included day and night
fighters, ground attack, anti-shipping, and high-altitude reconnaissance types. Top speed for a Nick, as listed in *Jane's Air-*

craft, was 340 miles per hour, with a service ceiling of 35,200 feet. For a photographic high-altitude mission, the aircraft was lightened by eliminating the forward-firing armament. Only the tail gunner/radio operator in the rear enclosed cockpit was armed. The gunner manned a swivel-mounted 7.7-mm machine gun, which could be rotated on a metal track.

Sketchy information obtained after the war revealed that, with the removal of all armor and the forward-firing guns and with modification of the engine's supercharger ratios, the Nick could attain an altitude in excess of forty thousand feet. This was ideal for photo reconnaissance, as it could now fly above all antiaircraft fire and most enemy fighters. The exact number of Nicks thus modified is unknown but could have been, at best, only four or five.

For several days prior to May 10 and always at first light, the modified Nick would appear over the fleet anchorage off Okinawa. After leisurely filming the mass of assembled ships, sometimes completing two great circles, the pilot would confidently head back to the Japanese home islands with film of the latest U.S. Navy ship positions. With the daily approach of dusk, every man aboard his vessel knew that kamikazes would soon be on their own way to certain death, often taking with them many U.S. servicemen. History has shown how terribly effective the dreaded kamikazes were.

The advent of the kamikazes inspired several changes in U.S. tactics, of which perhaps the courageous and sacrificial actions of the perimeter-guarding picket ships received the most notice. But there was another change in tactics, which this story relates, in response to the U.S. Fleet's predicament.

CAPT. KENNETH L. REUSSER, USMC, led his four pilots of VMF-312 in a running rendezvous, his position lights temporarily providing visual aid for the join-up. Flying on his wing was 1st Lt. Robert Klingman. The second section of Corsairs was led by 1st Lt. Jim Cox, and on his wing, flying as "Tail-end Charlie," was 1st Lt. Frank Watson. Their standard early-morning combat air patrol mission had been modified at Ken Reusser's request and approved by his commanding officer. Ken's flight, designated Red Flight, was going after the Japanese intruder.

Red Leader's idea was to be on station at maximum altitude when the high-altitude photo plane was first sighted. Otherwise, he would be long departed by the time any U.S. plane could take off, climb to altitude, and give pursuit. Reusser knew that the Corsair could not match the Nick's altitude, but he had made some preparations earlier that he hoped would improve their chances of getting close enough to shoot down the photo plane.

He had lightened the F4U in every way possible, reducing the .50-caliber machine gun ammunition to less than a hundred rounds per gun. He had also endured the smiles of the ground crews who watched as he had carefully waxed and rewaxed his aircraft the two previous days.

As the flight gained altitude and the light improved, ground control advised of an incoming bogey.

"Right on time," Reusser radioed his division. "We'll stay on the inside of his turn. I don't think he can see us against the water."

"Tally-ho the bogey." This was from section leader Jim Cox. "He's conning." The vapor trails were now clearly visible to all in the flight.

"Red Flight, max power, jettison tanks," Reusser ordered.

After a few moments, "Red Leader from Red Three. Tanks away but can you ease power a bit? My cylinder head temp is almost pegged."

"That's a negative, Red Three. We'll never catch him without full power. Red Two and Four, check in."

"This is Red Two. I'm OK but behind you a little. Engine is overheating but not too badly."

"Roger, Two. How about you, Red Four?"

"Sorry, Ken, this bird just can't take this power climb."

"OK, Red Three and Four, return to base. Acknowledge. Over."

"Roger" came through from each wingman, and now the odds were two to one. Still climbing and in high blower (supercharger), the two Corsairs in trail were turning inside the Nick's flight path as the Japanese pilot began a second orbit over the giant fleet far below. The pilot was apparently oblivious of the two marines trying desperately to overtake him.

"Red Two, I don't know. I'm only showing about two hundred FPM climb. It'll take a month to catch him at this rate."

"Roger, Red One," from Klingman. "I'm about a mile in trail behind you. You've sure got the best engine."

"But not enough, I'm afraid. Red Two, I'm going to try something. If I can pull enough lead angle, I'll spray the fifties. Maybe he'll do something stupid."

So saying, Ken leveled off slightly to pick up a little more speed. After a few moments, he eased back on the stick and squeezed the trigger. His lead angle was, in his words, "about two city blocks." The tracers arced out, traveling as if in slow motion to a spot well in front of the Nick. Several telltale glints on the surface of the Japanese plane announced that some strikes had hit.

"I think I hit him! Did you see those flashes?"

"Affirmative, affirmative!" from Red Two.

The two pilots watched with fascination, waiting for something to happen. Slowly the Nick turned and headed north for Japan, almost simultaneously beginning a very gradual descent. This was, of course, what the two marines had been hoping for, as did the entire fleet below. Unbeknownst to

Red Flight, the combat information centers on each ship that carried the appropriate VHF crystals were breathlessly following the aerial action on their loudspeakers.

As Reusser closed in on the Nick from directly behind, he could see a hole in the top of the right wing and some fluid or smoke trailing from the left engine. At point-blank range he again pressed the trigger. Nothing happened. His guns had finally frozen from the intense cold of the high altitude. This was not an uncommon occurrence, and Ken had already worked out an alternate plan.

Carefully maneuvering his Corsair directly under and behind the Nick, where he was sure he could not be spotted by either the pilot or the gunner, he inched closer to the enemy's tail surfaces. Adding throttle carefully, he closed the gap until the propeller began to neatly chew away the trailing edges of the tail surfaces. Immediately, the Nick pilot made several quick turns.

The element of surprise was gone now, and the elevator and rudder control surfaces had not been damaged enough to cause the enemy pilot to lose control of the aircraft.

"This is Red One. I tried to chop off his tail after my guns froze. Red Two, shoot him down—he's all yours."

"Roger, Red One, but my guns are frozen, too. I just tried them."

Reusser now pulled up on the right wing of the Japanese aircraft, and the two pilots, along with the gunner, stared at each other, eyeball to eyeball, less than fifty feet apart. The Japanese crew's thoughts would be unknown forever, and Reusser wondered afterward how many U.S. and Japanese pilots had actually flown formation together in World War II.

"I think this guy's convinced I'm alone, Red Two. Why don't you give it a go while I keep him occupied? He seems fascinated with my nice tight-wing position."

Then Reusser moved into a position where his left wing actually overlapped the Nick's right wing, effectively blocking any evasive turns. While the Japanese pilot seemed mesmerized, the gunner was not, as he frantically beat his fists on the machine gun while attempting to recharge and fire his weapon.

The cold air had affected all of the combatants equally in this high-altitude drama. Reusser watched as Klingman closed from underneath in the astern six o'clock position. Shortly, small amounts of flying debris told the same story as before. Red Two had gently and clinically done the same superficial damage as Red Leader. The Japanese pilot again banked away momentarily but then resumed his resolute course toward his home base. The Japanese mainland was getting closer by the minute.

"Let me try again, Red One. If I hit him too hard, we're both in the drink. Why didn't they give us better training for this tail-chopping maneuver?"

"Roger, Two. I'll stay on his wing and keep his attention if you want one more try. He must think his gunner is going to get that gun working. If he does, he won't miss you at this range. And we may not have enough fuel to get back from here, you know."

"That's a roger," from Red Two. "OK, here goes nothing!"

Klingman added power and climbed upward, aiming for a point just aft of the gunner's cockpit. The huge Hamilton Standard four-bladed prop ripped through the tail surfaces and on into the greenhouse.

The Nick's machine gun and its geared track disintegrated, as did the helpless gunner. Parts of the gunner and of both aircraft trailed out behind Red Two into the slipstream, slowly falling toward the ocean.

"I'm headin' for home, Red One. It's vibrating pretty bad,

At the airfield in Okinawa on 10 May 1945, Capt. Ken Reusser (*standing*) and 1st Lt. Bob Klingman on the wing of Klingman's Corsair. Note the damage to the wing and the missing propeller tip. *courtesy of Ken Reusser*

and I've only got about fifty gallons left. I don't think we'll make it."

"OK, Red Two. I'm right behind you. Got you in sight. Set up the best glide at the lowest RPM you can manage. The Nick is in a graveyard spiral and pieces are still flying off in all directions. Oh yeah! There goes a wing. Cancel one Jap photo mission. Nice going, Bob!"

The long ride home was exciting, exhilarating, and satisfying for both pilots. Klingman's aircraft ran out of fuel on the long straight-in approach, but he managed to land, as they say, "dead-stick." The plane was a total strike. Ken landed with only a few gallons of gasoline remaining.

A reenactment of the previous photograph, taken on 10 May 1995—exactly fifty years later. This time their positions are reversed, and Colonel Reusser sports the checkerboard scarf of VMF-312.

The Japanese daylight photo missions had ended. The kamikaze pilots' briefings were now incomplete, as the enemy could no longer pinpoint the exact locations of the U.S. capital ships.

Both Captain Reusser and First Lieutenant Klingman were subsequently awarded the Navy Cross for their gallant and heroic actions, but Captain Reusser's war was not over yet.

7 Coast to Coast in a '37 Piper Cub

M Y FIRST CAR was an airplane. My first real cross-country flight was more than three thousand miles long. The year was 1947, and my partner in this venture, William A. Poe, and I had decided to buy an old junker, fix it up a little, and fly it ocean to ocean from Jacksonville, Florida, to Claremont, California.

We both had been recently commissioned and were proudly wearing our Navy Wings of Gold as twenty-year-old Marine Corps second lieutenants. Bill and I had already received orders to report to the Marine Corps air station at El Toro, California, in four weeks. Incongruously, we were at the same time flying the famed F4U Corsairs, the gull-winged fighters of World War II, boasting almost 2,250 horsepower.

We felt that, as aviators (albeit brand-new ones), we should disdain the train as mundane and be more adventuresome . . . like buy our own airplane and fly it to the West Coast. The bus was never considered and neither of us owned, or for that matter had ever owned, a car. We chose an older model

"And there I was at 90,000 feet"

Six new Marine pilots who have just completed operational training in F4Us at Cecil Field in Florida on 1 September 1947. *Left to right:* Harvey Neilsen, Red Baker, Don Tooker, Bill Poe, Jim Morgan, Bill Miller, and Bob Welch, the instructor.

of aircraft for one reason only: It was all we could afford. By some shrewd manipulations we had pooled a fast $480. We had responded eagerly to an ad in the base newspaper for a 1937 Piper Cub, $600, as is. Upon close inspection we discovered "as is" meant it needed considerable work. The airport manager called it a sacrifice and said that it wasn't due for the required CAA (now FAA) annual inspection until December, it then being September. The wings had just been re-covered, but some cow, who apparently lived near the airport, had thoughtlessly put a hoof through the elevator. The fuselage fabric was pretty much in shreds. We chalked that up as inconsequential, since an airtight fuselage was not necessary for actual flight, as the very early flying machines attested.

The 1937 Cubs, having no electrical system, hence had no starters, no lights, and no radios. Hand-propping was required to start the engine. Most importantly, there were no brakes of any kind, only large sausage tires, which we counted on to slow down the aircraft when taxiing and after landings. This latter item would cause us some grief before long. Initially, the missing window on the left side of the cockpit appeared to be a problem. However, we rationalized that, in the humid Florida weather, the added ventilation compensated for the lack. We then applied the famous Peggy Lee Theory: "Who needs a window on such a sunny day?" and all was right with the world.

On the plus side of the ledger, the Little Clunker, as we affectionately called her, did have one liquid directional compass, an altimeter, an airspeed indicator, and an oil pressure gauge, which stuck occasionally. The precision gas gauge was a metal wire with a small loop at the top that was attached vertically through the center of the gas cap to a floating cork inside the nine-gallon fuel tank. When the wire loop end descended to the top of the gas cap, it would definitely be time to land. An air-driven turn and bank indicator rounded out our wealth of avionics.

After once around the small grass field, followed by a successful landing by Bill, we informed the airport manager that our total investment capability was limited to $480. His initial response was "Impossible," but when we slowly walked away, he caught up with us and the deal was struck. He even threw in a month's free tie-down and two cans of thirty-cent oil.

In the two weeks before our westward departure, we learned (on the job) how to recover the tail surfaces with a

The only known photograph of the 1937 Cub, taken at Cable Claremont Airport. A friend of the author poses for the Brownie camera shot.

special kind of linen and how to apply the many coats of dope needed to ensure the proper tautness. An old navy chief from the bi-wing rigging days helped us refinish and balance the wooden propeller. Once this was done, some of the annoying vibration disappeared. The final imperfection, however, was unfixable, at least by us. One of the four engine exhaust manifold studs was missing from the 50-horsepower Continental engine. The remaining three were certainly adequate from a safety standpoint, but the noise generated sounded like a car with a defective muffler. The resultant "flap-flap" sound would invariably cause people on the ground to stop and look up, startled by the unusual sound. Even livestock tended to become a little restless when we winged our way overhead.

The big day finally dawned. Almost forty well-wishers and skeptics, along with a contingent of the generally curious, came out to the field to see us off. The crowd consisted mainly of navy and Marine Corps pilots, all flying the F4U Corsair fighters. We detected in them a certain fascination for the unlikelihood of our small plane making the transcontinental dash successfully, particularly at the breakneck speed of fifty miles per hour.

There were numerous goodbye gifts, but our tiny baggage area behind the rear tandem seat allowed room only for our caps (we were in uniform), shaving kits, and a change of shirts, socks, and underwear—and Bill's box of graham crackers. We also squeezed in a pair of pliers and the two bonus quarts of thirty-cent oil. How critical the latter might become never occurred to either of us. The one farewell gift we did take with us was a small pamphlet, "Survival in the Jungle," by Frank Buck, thoughtfully provided by one of our pilot friends.

At 0745, 15 September 1947, second lieutenants Poe and Tooker rolled down the grass strip, lurched into the air, and took up a heading of due west out of Jacksonville. Our destination lay 3,100 miles away. Had we known what lay ahead, we might have reconsidered the train ride, lackluster or not. I don't know how Bill felt, but I was thinking about those other aviation pioneers—like Eddie Rickenbacker, Jimmy Doolittle, "Wrong Way" Corrigan . . . on second thought, not Corrigan.

With gas for three and a half to four hours, we could cruise comfortably for about 180 to 220 miles, depending upon the wind. We had two sets of maps: one set of U.S. aeronautical sectional charts (courtesy of the U. S. Government) and one set of road maps (courtesy Shell Oil Company). The latter were particularly valuable in that we always flew along the highways to lessen the risk of getting lost. From our normal cruising altitude of a thousand to twenty-five hundred feet we could see ahead only about eight to ten miles, but this allowed us to make out the town names painted on most water towers, a holdover from the barnstorming days of the twenties and thirties.

Our first preplanned stop was the Tallahassee Municipal Airport. We made this a lunch stop, although neither of us was particularly hungry. We refueled, checked the weather forecast, and flipped a coin to see who would fly the next leg. Bill won, leaving me the responsibilities of navigator, flight engineer, and stewardess. We left the capital of Florida completely confident that we could handle the next three thousand miles with no sweat. We climbed straight out of the field after receiving a green light from the tower and resumed the familiar heading of 270 degrees. Sitting in the rear seat, I settled back and occupied myself by alternately staring at the ant-like cars below and at the back of Bill's head. He needed a haircut. Somewhere in this fascinating process I dozed off to sleep. Once I got used to it, the steady "flap-flap" of the engine was not so bad.

About two hours later, I was awakened by a gentle tapping on my knee to see a look of anxiety on Bill's usually smiling face. He pointed to the wire loop sitting firmly on top of the gas cap. We did not have much longer to stay in the air. Next, he handed me the trusty Shell road map with a big x marking our position. It was obvious that we could not reach our next refueling stop. Headwinds of almost thirty miles an hour had slowed our forward progress to bicycle speed. Characteristically, Bill—as always, the career non-alarmist—had not bothered to disrupt my nap regarding this trivial matter until it had reached the crisis stage.

"What about those auxiliary fields we've marked on the charts?" I shouted.

"They're abandoned, I'm sure," Bill responded. "There won't be any refueling facilities. Of course, we can land OK and hitchhike to the nearest town, but then we'd never make Pensacola today."

Bill was right. If we set down on any one of the old military training fields, we'd be safe but stuck. We were still over the highway that stretched straight ahead for miles. I noted that the road had power lines on only one side.

"Are there any filling stations ahead? Haven't we passed some?"

"Yeah, but they were quite a way back. This headwind has been killing our ground speed," Bill went on to explain. "We picked it up about half an hour out of Tallahassee."

"OK, Bill, why don't you start down? It's always better to land with power. The road is a little narrow, but the traffic doesn't look too bad." No reply from Bill, as he eased back the throttle.

We could always get some help from a passing motorist, I thought to myself.

"There are some buildings up ahead, Don. One of them looks like it might be a gas station." It was.

After a quick 360-degree circle for a car-traffic check, Bill cut the power and made a nice three-point landing on the asphalt two-lane highway. He then taxied the Piper Cub J-3 across the neatly raked gravel and up to the lone gas pump, cutting the switches as I leaped out to ensure that we didn't run into the pump.

No one came out to greet our unheralded arrival. I walked over to the front of a building that looked like a general store. A large sign announced that we were about to do business with Charlie's Flying-A Service Station. After I had knocked several times, the top half of a Dutch door opened cautiously and a bearded man in greasy overalls peered out at me with bovine indifference.

"Can we buy some gas here?" I inquired. "Do you have any ethyl?"

"No, just regular. Help yourself. It's eighteen cents a gallon. Be sure and refill the pump when you're done." I helped Bill pump in the almost nine gallons from the glass-walled, gravity-fed pump, even in 1947 something of a relic.

"Where's the owner?" Bill asked.

"He's inside. I don't know why he's not coming out."

"Did he say anything? Ask any questions?"

"No, Bill. Apparently he has aircraft refueling here everyday. He must be tired of so many pilots passing through."

I ignored Bill's quizzical look and put $1.62 on a desk just inside of the door of Charlie's Flying-A Air Terminal. The old man never did come out. His apparent lack of interest in our emergency refueling stop remains a puzzlement to this day.

Reluctant to overstay our welcome, we dragged the plane back, away from the pump stand. Bill hand-propped the engine into life and jumped into the seat behind me. After waiting several minutes for the automobile traffic to clear, I scattered Charlie's driveway gravel all over with the prop blast and took off down the road toward Pensacola.

"If this wind will die down a little, we'll make Pensi just about dusk," I shouted to Bill. He nodded as he measured the remaining miles on our chart. But the wind did not let up, and our forward progress at cruising altitude was just a shade faster than that of the grazing cattle below. We dropped down to a hundred feet to escape the headwind, but still the cars were zipping by us.

"Don, we aren't going to make it. We'll need another fuel stop to get there." Bill was right again. I had been watching for more filling stations, now as a ho-hum routine source of fuel, but they had petered out, leaving only a lonely stretch of road to watch.

"There's Eglin Air Force Base up ahead," Bill reported, "only it's a SAC Base. Prior permission to land required, and emergencies don't count."

"Will they shoot us if we land there?" I asked, facetiously.

"Probably. They don't like marines anyway." As the air force base hove into view, I made a decision, based in part on my new role as an aircraft owner and in part on the tempting proximity of fuel, which I did not want to run out of.

"Let's land on a taxiway and then motor up to Airfield Operations. Surely they'll see we are not going to take over their field." I received an affirmative nod from the other aircraft owner in the back seat.

"Bill, this is the airfield where Doolittle trained his B-25 group in 1942 for the Tokyo Raid." He ignored that.

I changed heading slightly and lined up on the narrow taxiway paralleling the huge ten-thousand-foot runway. There was no other traffic in sight. We touched down smoothly and proceeded to taxi in a westerly direction toward the control tower and Airfield Operations. Suddenly, a command vehicle appeared in front of us, effectively blocking our path. Behind this vehicle was a jeep with an airman crouched over a .50-caliber machine gun aimed directly at us.

"I think they want us to stop," Bill said. A loudhailer boomed as two uniformed men jumped to the ground, crouching menacingly, each cradling a Thompson submachine gun.

"Shut down your engine and disembark immediately with your hands up!"

We did just that, as it really seemed like the thing to do. For about three or four minutes no one moved. We put on our marine uniform caps and tried to look official. A military sedan appeared momentarily and a young-looking major wearing a sidearm got out and walked over to our airplane.

"Just what in the hell are you guys doing? You can't land here, this is a SAC base!"

We explained our emergency fuel state, showed him our ID cards at his behest, and offered him a copy of our orders. He relaxed a very small amount and then told his airmen to stand easy, which apparently meant not to point the machine guns *directly* at us. He informed us that we would have to take off immediately to avoid certain unspecified consequences. I asked if he was a pilot, looking directly at his silver wings.

"Of course. What's that got to do with it?" I mentioned something about one pilot ordering another to an almost certain forced landing and possibly a serious crash. He looked at me for a long hard minute and then went over to the jeep, where he conversed on the radio for several minutes. He returned with a slightly softer attitude.

"OK, here's what I'm going to do." Pointing to me: "Lieutenant, you get in my sedan. She'll drive you to the base service station. They'll loan you a five-gallon gas can. You pay for the gas and come directly back here. That should be enough gas to get you to Pensacola."

The WAC driver delivered me to the service station, where I filled the borrowed gas can. I was following orders very carefully, as only a new second lieutenant operating within a firing-squad scenario can do. In fifteen minutes we were back at the plane. The gum-chewing lady driver seemed fascinated with the entire scene but never spoke one word. She had exceeded the base speed limits in each of the restricted zones, but I magnanimously declined to put her on report.

We made a funnel from one of the road maps, and the

major himself climbed up on the sausage tire and poured the entire five gallons into the tank, without spilling a drop.

"Now, you Jarheads, get into your plane, take off to the west, and if you turn back in this direction, I'll shoot you down personally. I'm keeping a copy of your USMC orders, and if I hear that you've even mentioned landing here at Eglin, I'll inform your commandant of your blatant disregard of regulations!"

We took off immediately, as ordered. We did not turn back even for an instant and have kept the lid on this serious infraction, as ordered. The base is closed now, but Bill and I would never go back there . . . just in case.

The wind finally died down as the sun set in front of us. We landed safely, albeit at great risk, in total darkness at Stump Field. Our approach to the grass field was relatively easy. Anyone interested in duplicating it should fly down the main road that leads to Mainside, then turn right at the drive-in movie, closing the throttle. This maneuver would put the aircraft right into the middle of a blackness called Stump Field.

At least that's how we did it.

We tied the Little Clunker down and caught a local bus for the bachelor officers quarters at the naval air station. It had been a routine day of flying: twelve hours in the air, two emergency landings for fuel, and a night landing on an unlighted field surrounded by trees on four sides. What would tomorrow hold?

It turned out that our friends, whom we had called from Jacksonville earlier that morning, had waited for us at the field, but they had left after dark because they *knew* we couldn't make the landing without lights.

At the club that evening we had a great time, graciously accepting any and all free drinks and good-luck toasts. We told and retold the highway refueling episode to an appreciative audience. The SAC base incident, however, was never discussed.

A marine friend took us out to our airplane the next morning at 0600, and we took off for a short run to Mobile, Alabama, there being enough fuel left over from the Eglin service station refueling. The Stump Field proprietor never knew he had had such famous overnight visitors, and we had saved a one-dollar tie-down fee.

The Mobile Municipal Airport has an exciting aircraft parking area. Upon departing the landing runway, the taxiway descends 100 to 150 feet down a gentle incline, with hangars on the left and the aircraft tie-down area on the right. After our landing, with me at the controls, we started down the incline to the refueling and parking area. We were always prepared to execute our braking procedure, whereby one of us got out of the cockpit, grabbed the wing strut, and dragged his feet to slow the plane. Upon the command, "Brakes," Bill jumped out as we slowly headed down to the parking area and planted his feet. However, Bill's "brakes" failed; the soles and heels of his uniform low-cut shoes were leather. They worked fine on grass, but the paved taxiway was a whole different problem. No traction!

"Kill the switches, Don! I can't stop her!"

I shut off the magnetos and then watched, horrified, as we crashed into a pretty red and white Stinson Voyager. In the ensuing embarrassing silence, I got out, wondering how much it would cost to get out of this one.

"You fellers don't have brakes on that bird, do you?" asked a bewiskered older man who was obviously a well-seasoned aircraft mechanic.

"No, Sir," was all either of us could muster. The three of us untangled the two mated aircraft and then examined the wings of the attacking Piper Cub and the offended Stinson.

There was absolutely no visible damage to the Stinson, just a slight yellow smudge that wiped off easily. The right leading edge of our bird was stove in for almost three feet.

"It'll never fly again," Bill lamented. I was too chagrined even to comment.

The mechanic, who looked as though he had just stepped out of an old Wallace Beery movie, didn't seem too upset. He disappeared into a hangar and was back in a few moments carrying a long piece of bailing wire. He dragged a toolbox over to our damaged wing. Stepping up onto the box, with pliers he bent one end of the wire into a gentle curve like the letter C. Picking up a small hand-cranked drill, he made a tiny hole about the size of the wire into the leading edge of the Cub's wing. He then inserted the curved end of the wire and magically popped out the concave portion of the wing's leading edge. Next, he covered the hole with a piece of cloth tape and, almost with a flourish, then applied a dab of fabric dope. He refused any money but did give two newly enlightened, high-performance fighter pilots a short lecture on how to taxi a brakeless airplane on paved surfaces. We never made that mistake again; others, maybe.

With Mobile behind us and once again airborne, Bill set in our exact magnetic heading on our sensitive, state-of-the-art compass by turning west. While Bill cleverly manipulated the exquisitely complicated Piper Cub controls, I borrowed Bill's shave kit for a pillow and made off to sleep. About three hours later, we rolled to a stop in Gulfport, Mississippi. We had averaged over eighty miles per hour, setting a new speed record for marine pilots flying Piper Cubs during the middle of the week in September. How fickle the winds could be. We had tailwind now, but the headwinds of yesterday had nearly done us in.

The weather was absolutely perfect as we took off again

and headed for Moisant International Field in Louisiana. The beaches along the Gulf of Mexico were clean, bright, dazzling white. Bordering the sand, the deep blue-green ocean was so clear we could easily make out the bottom several hundred feet from shore. We could see many fish and several sharks of good size, which tended to discourage us from flying very far out over the water. We followed the coastline for two more hours and then easily identified the large body of water ahead as Lake Pontchartrain, just to the north of New Orleans.

The runways were intimidatingly long, so we landed on a grassy area in front of a hangar with a sign that said ELEV. 400. (In 1947 you could get away with a lot of things that would be severely frowned upon today.) We filled our empty tank with eighty-octane gasoline, checked the oil, and purchased a lovely lunch-to-go: two Delaware Punches, some sandwiches, and two very stale cupcakes. A quick visit to an outhouse behind the hangar completed the necessary defueling part of the rest stop. All this and we were airborne again in only fifteen minutes. After a slight hesitation, we chose our next heading: West.

It was my turn to play pilot, so Bill was relegated to the back seat.

"Pilot to navigator. Be sure your safety belt is firmly secured and that your seat back is in the upright position, because in a minute we're going to go really fast!"

Bill's vacant stare told me he didn't understand commercial airliner talk. I continued my ramblings.

"In the event of a water landing, you may use your seat cushion as a flotation device. You must then kick your little feet." Another dull stare.

My efforts to liven up the trip were unappreciated by the navigator, but the weather changed abruptly and immediately erased any possible boredom. For the next two and a half hours we changed altitudes and wove in and around the rainy tunnels formed by huge towering cumulous clouds. They were beautiful, awe-inspiring, and dangerous, particularly for lightplanes. We did as small car owners do when challenged by large trucks: We yielded the right of way with a minimum loss of prestige.

Onward we flew. Below us now were hundreds of tiny shimmering lakes surrounded by dense green bayous. Into these beautiful yet deadly swamps, many an aviator has made his final landing. Few roads lead in, and none lead out, as the saying goes. Flying at a few hundred feet to avoid the turbulence of the storm clouds, we could see the sun's occasional reflections on the tangled undergrowth that edged the many small ponds. Here and there the road that we were following would make a sharp turn or detour around some impenetrable area, which we courageously cut across to save time. During these shortcuts, my grip on the throttle would invariably tighten slightly.

"Getting low on gas, Bill."

"OK, I'll have a field for you shortly." I thought I heard him add, "I hope."

"Over there, Don, just to the right of those tracks and north of town." Old Graham Cracker Breath was right; it was our field.

The town of Jennings, Louisiana, is nowhere in particular (apologies to the residents of Jennings) but it was a welcome sight to us, complete with grass field and windsock. The strip was soaked from the present and recent rains, but our balloon tires this time were an advantage.

From Jennings to Port Arthur, I had nothing to do but dry off and watch the tiny droplets of oil trickling back from the engine over the nose cowling and along the fuselage until they disappeared from sight. The engine was suffering from "rocker-arm-itis," according to Bill.

"Nothing to worry about," he had assured me, "all old engines throw some oil." It was fine with me, as long as the engine knew it was all right to throw oil.

We sailed into Port Arthur during another deluge of pouring rain. The field resembled a swimming pool, except there were no diving boards at either end. We landed with a splash rather than a touchdown. I had become convinced by now that Bill and I owned a real, live amphibian aircraft; we just had not realized that when we bought it.

We refueled in the rain by borrowing a canvas tarp to cover us while we put in the gasoline. We did not need any water in the gas tank to make our journey more challenging. No other aircraft were flying or, for that matter, even moving around the field. The water was six inches deep in places, tending to discourage those pilots who knew better.

Houston, our final destination for the day, was less than two hours away, so we bade a tearful farewell to the other planes sitting there in the mud and took off for drier endeavors, we hoped. Several doubters did come out of the hangars to see with their own eyes our attempt at taking off from their lake. With water spraying in every direction, we splashed down the underwater strip and staggered into the air without incident. The only real casualties were our expensive cordovan military shoes. They were a soggy, sorry mess.

The airfield was wonderfully dry when we landed at Sam Houston Airport, just as the sun was setting. We had chosen this airport on the advice of a navy commander at Cecil Field, Florida. He had learned to fly at this small grass field before the war in 1940. He had also bragged on how friendly the folks were that ran the FBO (Fixed Base Operation). The commander spoke with straight tongue. After we'd refueled and tied down the Little Clunker, we located the airport manager to ask his recommendations regarding possible sleeping arrangements.

"I know a pretty good place," he said, quite hospitably. "The Claridge Hotel. It's old but clean, kind of a family-type hotel with mostly permanent residents. They serve dinner and breakfast, too."

We accepted his offer of a ride into town and piled into the manager's car, a 1941 Ford sedan that still had a wartime "B" gas rationing sticker on the windshield. He told us his name was Cliff Hyde and that he had been in the airplane flying business since the early thirties.

"You boys must be a little tired. You said you'd been airborne thirteen hours today?"

"Yes, Sir," Bill replied. "We took off from a field in Pensacola right at six o'clock this morning."

We told Cliff our plans and that we expected to reach California in two more days. He was impressed but was a lot more so when we told him we made our living flying Corsairs. He'd been an Army Air Corps pilot in World War II, flying L-5s, observation aircraft used to spot artillery fire.

Arriving at the hotel, our newfound friend offered to pick us up in the morning for the return ride to the airport. Of course we accepted. After inquiring within, we learned that there *was* room at the inn. The old gentleman at the front desk welcomed us warmly.

"I've got a son in the army," he beamed. "Glad to have you boys stay with us. We still offer a military discount. It'll be $3.50 each plus a dollar more if you want dinner."

"Can't beat that," Bill responded. "What time is dinner and what time do you serve breakfast?" I was somewhat relieved that Bill had not seen fit to straighten out the proprietor on the vital fact that we were *marines,* not army men.

"Kitchen stays open till eight-thirty. You'd best wash up and get back down here. I'll tell 'em they got two more coming. Kitchen opens at six for coffee and rolls." I silently hoped his remark about washing up before dinner was just a suggestion and had nothing to do with our thirteen hours in a cramped, tiny cockpit.

"Can we have a wake-up call?" I asked.

"Sure, the night man can knock on your door. We don't have phones in the rooms yet. What time would you like?"

"Five-thirty would be fine," I replied. "But please make sure we each come to the door; otherwise, we'll just roll over and go back to sleep."

Bill and I climbed up the stairs, there being no elevator, carrying our minuscule personal kits. He was stationed on the second floor, me on the third. How propitious this would be.

"Let's meet in the dining room in half an hour, Bill. I need a shower pretty bad." He was surprisingly quick to agree.

The room was quite small. A double bed was covered by a homemade quilted comforter. There was a desk and chair and a small vanity that also served as a closet, but no bathroom facilities. The $3.50-a-night price should have alerted me. No harm done. I grabbed a towel from the wall rack and, clutching my shave kit, struck out in search of the down-the-hall john. Sure enough, at the end of the hall was a door clearly marked BATHROOM. It was unlocked, so I entered.

There should have been an OCCUPIED sign posted, because it was very much occupied, with an attractive naked lady sitting in the bathtub. I came to an abrupt halt with mouth open but brain not engaged.

"Please excuse me," I finally blurted out. "You see the door wasn't locked, and . . . ."

"Oh, that's OK. They've been going to fix the darn lock for months." Her disarming smile relaxed me a little and I was almost able to breathe normally. A very good-looking brunette, particularly well endowed and about twenty-five years old, she was definitely not ill at ease

"I was looking for a shower. We've been flying all day." I tried not to sound too desperate to keep the conversation going.

"Well, there aren't any showers on this floor, only this one bathtub. I'll be finished in a few minutes and then it's yours." She paused for a moment while I tried both not to stare and to achieve a smattering of nonchalance. "How long are you staying with us?"

"Only for one night, I'm afraid. We're on our way to the West Coast, my copilot and I."

"How exciting! Me, I'm on my way to a party. Say . . . are you in a partying mood? There'll be some other pilots there, I'm sure."

"If that's an invitation, thanks, but I'm really pooped. Right now dinner and a bed sound pretty good." I couldn't believe what I was hearing me say. A virile, twenty-year-old marine pilot was turning down a party with a young and pretty lady he had just met in a bathtub?

"Well, too bad. Hope you sleep well," she said, a little sarcastically. "Are you in 311?" I nodded yes, sadly realizing that our sparking conversation was drawing to a close.

"If I get home at a reasonable hour, maybe I'll see if you're still up." I nodded again and wondered if she would be too upset if I hung around while she let out the bath water.

"Talk to you later" was the best departing line I could muster. In five minutes the bathroom was available. After a quick bath and a change of underwear, presto! I was a new man.

Dinner was on the table, and Bill had already started eating.

"How was your shower?" he asked. "Mine ran out of hot water."

"They only have a bathtub on my floor." I considered through most of the country-fried steak and green beans whether or not to share my bathroom adventure with him. He probably wouldn't believe me if I said something like, "I ran into a naked lady in the bathtub, and we had a nice chat. She asked me to a party, and I said I was too tired." Hell, I wouldn't have believed him if he had told *me* some story like that. We were truly exhausted and finished our dinner quickly.

"Let's meet in the lobby at ten to six," I suggested. "Cliff, the FBO guy, will undoubtedly be on time."

"OK, Don, see you at 0550."

We re-ascended the stairs and went to our respective rooms. I didn't know about Bill, but I was asleep in just moments, too tired to even dream.

A gentle knocking at the door signaled that morning had arrived. As requested, the knocking continued until I opened the door to assure the night man that I was really awake. The night man was short, brunette, and wearing a very cute black cocktail dress.

"You're still up," she smiled. Standing there in my Skivvies, I figured she must be pretty naive. Then I began to catch the drift, as the cobwebs of sleep vanished.

"Would you like to stop by? I live right next door in 310."

I responded with a now alert "yes" and closed the door. I quickly brushed my teeth, put back on my only clean tee-shirt and pulled on my uniform trousers. For a moment I looked for my watch but, on second thought, decided it didn't make any difference what time it was.

Her door was slightly ajar and the room smelled of some light tropical fragrance, like a cologne I remembered called "Balalaika." Closing the door behind me, I wondered what clever strategy would be appropriate. I needn't have given it a thought—she was already in bed waiting. I slipped off my trousers and shorts, forgetting my tee-shirt, and, trying very hard to act casually, eased into bed beside her. We made love enthusiastically and without conscience.

She was disappointed when I left almost immediately afterward, but as I tried to explain, I couldn't miss the five-thirty wake-up call.

Once I was back in my own bed, my last fleeting thought was, *Now I know Bill isn't going to believe this.* (It has been our little secret now for over fifty years, the Bathtub Lady's and mine.)

The next morning at exactly five-thirty the real night man woke me up, as promised. I dressed and after a quick shave met Bill and Cliff in the lobby, where both were finishing their coffee.

"You boys ready to get 'em in the air?" I had the feeling he was a little envious of our transcontinental endeavor.

"What's your next destination?"

"El Paso," Bill replied. The two got into the front seat while I closed my eyes in reflection in the back seat of the sedan. I couldn't help but relive the glandular episode of the previous evening. I hadn't even asked her name, but she hadn't asked for mine, either. *Wonder why she knocked at my door.* Perhaps it was my devilish good looks. Or maybe she had just plain struck out at the party. While debating these considerations, I drifted off.

"Come on, Don." Bill was practically dragging me out of the car. "We've got a lot of miles to cover. You look shot. Didn't you sleep well?"

"Not exactly. How about you taking the first leg?" I remembered that we would be flying all day and still be in the state of Texas.

Landing at Cameron was a first-time experience. I had

never slept through an approach and landing in a lightplane before. I had awakened from my little restorative nap just as we were taxiing in to the refueling pumps. It was quite a shock to have closed my eyes at three thousand feet and then suddenly to have opened them on the landing rollout.

After refueling, we traded jobs. Completely refreshed and refurbished, I now took my turn to shine as chief pilot. I notified all passengers to fasten seat belts for takeoff. The next order of business was to complete the detailed check-off list: (1) listen to hear if the engine was running, (2) look for other aircraft in the traffic pattern, and (3) check the grass strip for stray cattle. In most of Texas the open range policy was in effect, so cattle had the right of way. The weather was clear and warm and our spirits were high. Little did we expect the trouble that lay ahead.

After an uneventful pit stop at San Angelo, we were back in the air again. Next stop: Wink. It was still my turn up front, and we decided twenty-five hundred feet would be the optimum cruising altitude, windwise. How important this choice would be!

The scenery had changed from a verdant green to a tired, boring khaki brown, with scraggily sagebrush dotting the landscape below. It was strictly Shell-road-map navigation now, with pitifully few landmarks. The secondary road we were following abruptly made a right turn, north, for what seemed to be about twenty-five to thirty miles and then resumed the traditional westerly heading.

"What do you think, Bill? We can save almost twenty miles by cutting across. Wink is still a hundred and sixty miles away." The vote was close but unanimous. We decided to cut across. Although I really did have second thoughts, I was reluctant to admit that flying over some uncharted sagebrush was any big deal.

About halfway along the hypotenuse, the sun suddenly went out. Oil was everywhere, engulfing the windscreen in front and the windows along the right side of the aircraft. Only the left missing window provided any appreciable visibility.

"What happened?" Bill yelled. I had immediately retarded the throttle, making talking a bit easier. Unfortunately, it made maintaining altitude impossible.

"I think we've got a broken oil line. I knew we should have stayed over that road," I said, committing the kind of remark that neither eased the tension nor brightened our suddenly dimmed morale. Not being able to see forward made for a serious situation. I retarded the throttle further to conserve what oil remained. We had to come down, that was certain —but where?

"How much altitude do we have left?" asked Bill.

"Two thousand feet or a little less now." We had a few minutes of gliding before we would have to land. The missing left window was proving to be a godsend, since it was the only porthole of vision besides opening the door.

The seconds ticked by and with each one a few precious feet of altitude slipped away. This time our luck had really run out. There was no Army Air Corps major to bail us out. We both knew what a landing in sagebrush meant—usually a complete washout of the plane when it flipped over on its back.

"Find a dirt road or a building of some kind," Bill instructed from the back seat. "What's our oil pressure?"

"You don't want to know." Bill didn't need to know that it wasn't showing much of anything, hovering just above the zero mark. Searching frantically through the opaque windscreen was like trying to see through glass brick with peanut butter smeared on it for good measure.

"One thousand feet," I informed Bill.

"Yeah." His face had that pallbearer's fixed expression. I began tightening the small lap belt for what I knew was to come. Now I was sorry we had not told anyone of our exact route. As I cinched up the safety belt, I let go of the stick momentarily, causing a shallow turn to the right. We had been holding a steady westerly course, hoping to cover as much ground as possible during our gliding descent and to increase the chances of spotting something, anything, that we could land on. A yell from Bill:

"Over there, farther to the right! There's a barn and another building. Looks like some kind of a small ranch."

"Roger, roger. I've got it in sight, but we've only got five hundred feet left."

Giving the Cub an encouraging blast with the throttle stopped our descent momentarily but covered the windshield with a fresh bath of brown oil. Bill broke the tense silence:

"With a little luck you might set her down in that green area behind the barn. It's some sort of corral, but that's the only clear area I see."

Bill's observation was correct. It was apparently the only feasible setting-down spot. But I would not have the luxury of a flyover to check out the landing area. It would be one approach, one landing, and, as the old cliché went, a landing we both might walk away from. The landing area we had selected was in the shape of a soup bowl, with steep sides and a path, not a road, that cut diagonally across the floor of the bowl. It was now obvious that this was a cow pasture, complete with residents.

Stretching a glide is an aviation no-no, but stretch we did. The landing area looked to be about three hundred feet long, like a football field without the goal posts, and with wall-like sides all round the periphery.

"Bill, be ready to jump out and dig in those cordovans. I'll cut the switches as soon as I see we can make it." He acknowledged by raising a thought that I had not yet considered.

"We may not to able to get out once we get in, Don." He was right, of course, but first things first. Tomorrow's breakfast decisions were not really germane at this moment.

Giving the engine one final, oil-spewing burst to clear the last uncharted clump of sagebrush, I cut the switches and concentrated on making a three-point, full-stall landing. I noticed several cows on both sides of us grazing unhurriedly as Bill opened the side door and reached out for the wing strut. The wheels touched down as I kicked the rudders gently to fishtail so as to help slow down. The bank at the far end was coming nearer and nearer.

"Plant 'em, Bill," I shouted. It was so quiet I could have whispered. As his feet hit the ground, the plane slowed immediately and then turned sharply to the right. A moment later we were stopped, faced in the opposite direction. We looked at each other for several minutes, there not being a whole lot to say. I was the first to speak:

"Great work, Bill. That was a world-class job of stopping." The braking specialist merely nodded as he tried to clean off his oily hands and the dust and dirt he had picked up. He was "behind-the-refrigerator" dirty.

"I had to lock my fingers around that strut or you'd have lost me a ways back."

Several cows were slowly making their way over to our end of our impromptu runway, obviously to check out their new visitors. The look of unconcern in their eyes told us that very possibly some of them were quite accustomed to seeing our particular model of Piper Cub J-3 land in their pasture. As I crawled out of the cockpit, I could see we had actually landed in a large bowl with sides so steep that fences were not needed to keep the cattle in their own backyard.

"Those *are cows,* aren't they?" Bill asked, with some anxiety.

"I think so," I replied. "Bulls have bigger horns than these guys. They're probably steers. We'd better keep 'em away or they'll use the plane to rub against. Wave your shirt at 'em."

Leaving my fighter pilot buddy stripped to the waist, madly waving his marine khaki shirt at the Texas livestock spectators, I proceeded to have a look at what might become our new home. As I glanced at the sides of the embankment, I allowed myself a brief pat on the back. The landing speed had been perfect. The rollout across some narrow wooden planking that bridged the cows' watering pond had been just enough to allow our team-braking actions to bring the Cub to a stop some twenty feet short of the hillside. But even with this bit of success, I was not quite ready to have my face carved on a mountainside. We still had to figure a way out.

Standing by the plane, Bill had apparently convinced his audience that the air show was over and was busily wiping off some of the oil with our one spare rag.

"Go find some more rags," he instructed, "and help me with this mess. Before we can fix the trouble, if it *can* be fixed, we've got some cleaning up to do."

I made my way up the steep incline and once on top, spotted a house and a barn with a shed-like structure attached, several hundred feet away. Just behind the barn, a tall, faded red silo stood sentinel-like, looking over the other farm buildings.

"Hallooo," I shouted, several times. There were no signs of any human activity, and after a few more vocal efforts, I decided to do a little reconnoitering. I found two dogs, both friendly, some white chickens intent on scratching for food, and a ragged old patchwork quilt hanging forlornly on a fence. Walking up to the house, I peered cautiously through the windows. There was no one inside. I then knocked on doors, whistled loudly, and in general made a substantial racket. Since we had seen no roads during our landing approach, it seemed odd that no people were about. Looking further, I located several horses in the barn chewing on some hay, but they could provide little information. A broken-down tractor inside the shed was equally uncommunicative.

Having fulfilled all the prevailing rules of Texas ranch visiting etiquette, I pulled the old quilt from its long-time resting place and headed back to our newly designated landing strip. We then both got involved in the cleanup detail, using the appropriated quilt. After several minutes, Bill spoke.

"Well, Don, I've found the trouble. One of the locking tabs on the oil filler cap has broken off. This must have let the oil cap vibrate open a half-turn or so. Then the pressure in the lubrication system was enough to force the oil out past the cap."

"Can we fix it, do you think?"

"No, not out here, I'm afraid," Bill responded. "We've got to assume that the locking mechanism will vibrate open again. The dipstick registers less than one quart. That's hardly enough to warm up the engine, much less get us airborne. But wait, we've got those two quarts that the guy back in Jacksonville gave us. Those two thirty-centers might just be our ticket out of here to beautiful Wink. That's a lot better than spending the winter here."

"By the way," my suddenly talkative copilot went on, "what or whom did you encounter up there on the high ground?"

While I explained the lack of any human inhabitants present, Bill made a funnel from the same road map the army major had used at the Eglin SAC base. Pouring carefully, he spilled none of the precious lubricant. The map, having done more than had ever been expected of it, was a total write-off.

"Less than three quarts, Don, but it should be enough. Thank God we don't have a high-performance engine." He paused a moment, then asked: "What about a replacement for the oil cap? We're not going very far without one."

"I haven't solved that little item yet, Bill. Do you think we could pound a hunk of that quilt into the filler neck? It might hold for awhile."

"That's negative. If it blew out ten miles down the road, we'd be right back in the hole again, only this time without a nice landing spot like this and no spare oil. No, I'd say we've got to find a better way."

I stood there, wanting to give Bill a more positive response than Grandma's old quilt. We could not afford another forced landing, for sure, and we both were beginning to wonder how much more luck we could reasonably expect. Then a sudden flood of brilliance surged over my brain cells.

"Bill, if you'll resume your cow guard duties, I may have an answer. No guarantee, but give me a minute."

So saying, I scaled the cows' prison walls once more and headed for the broken-down tractor. It hadn't moved. The oil cap was still attached but came off, grudgingly, under my highly motivated efforts. I fervently hoped that Mr. Henry Ford and Mr. Continental (aka Engine) had used the same supplier when purchasing oil tank caps.

"Here, Bill, try this one for size." He did, and it did . . . .fit!

"Where in the world did you find it? Don't tell me there's another Piper Cub up there?" I explained how we had *borrowed* one tattered quilt and now we were borrowing one Ford tractor oil cap. Bill readily agreed that our need for these items was greater than that of the present owners, wherever they were.

"You think we can get out of here?" Bill asked. "I don't think leaving one of us behind solves anything, although it would increase the likelihood of a successful takeoff. You said there was no one around the place. Did you see any telephone lines?"

"No, no wires or lines of any kind. And it doesn't look like the kind of neighborhood with underground utilities. There's probably a power generator around somewhere, but I didn't see one."

"Bill, I think I do have a plan. But with all my experience in lightplanes, which is was about ten hours total before this trip, I'm not exactly rolling in confidence that we can pull it off."

I explained the plan: "We'll clear off the rocks, cow dung, and debris from our takeoff path. Then we'll taxi down to the other end so as to take off into whatever wind there is, which appears to be out of the west. Since we've got no brakes, we'll have to find some stones just the right size to place in front of the tires. This'll allow us to rev up the engine to full throttle so as to jump the chocks just as we reach full power. That'll give us the shortest possible takeoff roll. And we either make it or we don't. What do you think?"

"I don't have a better plan. How much wind is there up above this bowl?"

"I'd say about eight to ten knots," I answered. "It's right into our takeoff direction once we clear that hill."

We shook hands solemnly, like two cavalry scouts about to gallop off into hostile territory. Bill propped the engine into life and I taxied slowly downward to the takeoff position, with Bill carefully policing the dirt path as we went. I had been elected to be the front pilot, perhaps because I had gotten us into the field originally. The logic of this escaped me, but then changing seats on the *Titanic* wouldn't have helped anybody much, either.

After experimenting several times with rocks too small, we finally located two perfectly smooth pasture stones that we could jump over at full throttle. Bill got in, buckled up, and slapped me on the shoulder.

"Let's go, Lindbergh!" With a roar and a wish, we powered up and leaped over the chocks, gathering speed quickly. I got the tail up immediately and then held the nose down to gain as much speed as possible. It took every bit of my concentration not to begin climbing too soon. The hillside was rushing at us, and at the last second I yanked back on the stick. We zoomed up and over the embankment, clearing the uncharted sagebrush by inches. But the sudden steep climb caused the plane to mush, with our forward progress resembling a stagger more than pure flight. For several minutes of barely flying, the issue was in doubt. Finally, we were climbing slowly as the wind gathered itself beneath our wings. I heard an audible sigh from the passenger in the back seat.

A quick circle of the ranch we'd just departed revealed no discernible roads, only some paths leading in no particular direction. We never figured out where the people were or how they commuted to wherever they traveled. We dipped a wing for the cows' benefit and headed west for Wink, promising ourselves never to leave the comfort and safety of paved highways again, shortcuts be damned. I wondered, briefly, who fed the dogs.

In about thirty minutes we picked up our friendly road, which we had left to save time, and took up a position directly over the centerline.

As the Wink airport hove into view, I could not help but review our recent takeoff. If we had taken off in the other direction and had not checked the wind first, we'd have ripped out some serious sagebrush and most certainly would have bent the airplane pretty badly, and maybe us pilots as well.

At Wink we refueled and switched pilots, added two quarts of oil, and cleaned up the Little Clunker with some genuine rags and gasoline. It still looked like little boys' dirty feet. We sighted down the highway for Salt Flat, 120 miles away. We, and most of the cars headed in that direction, made the trip in less than two hours. Tail winds can do that.

It was dusk when we rolled to a stop. Salt Flat had fuel but, in a word, it was no metropolis. It served only as an emergency landing field and as a navigational aid for those lucky enough to fly with instruments. The gentleman caretaker who sold us the gas told us in which direction El Paso lay— west. We must have impressed him as pilots who were perhaps uncertain of things. He was amazed to learn that we had departed Jacksonville, Florida, two days earlier and were headed for California. Apparently our transportation did not fit his idea of a suitable cross-country vehicle.

"Only a hundred miles to go, Don," Bill informed me from the front seat. "Let's go hit the big city lights of El Paso." Since we were now seasoned night flyers, it seemed like the right thing to do. Besides, the huge ten-thousand-foot runways there were sure to be lighted.

As we approached the bright lights of the city, identifiable from at least fifty miles away, it became apparent that the International Airport manager had not paid his electric bill. The field was dark, and it was a full hour after sunset. He could not see us either, because we had no lights—not even a flashlight.

"Shall we just sneak in or what?" I asked Bill. He ignored my doorknob intelligence while he began a slow orbit east of the field and pondered the situation. We were not going back to lovely Salt Flat, even though we had enough fuel. Things were getting a bit desperate, and the darkness seemed threatening. Suddenly, the runway lights flashed on and everything lit up like a WCTU-approved cocktail bar.

"Guess they must have heard our flap-flap engine," Bill explained. But he was mistaken because, off to our right a little way, two pencil-like beams of light knifed into the night and shot down to the west landing runway. This meant only one thing: A big commercial airliner was about to land.

"We're in luck, Don. Now we *can* sneak in. We'll just follow him in and go wherever he goes." In a few minutes we were bumping along the runway in the wake turbulence of a four-engine DC-6. He parked near the control tower while we continued on to a hangar marked VISITING AIRCRAFT. We located a mechanic and had him unlock the gas pump so that we could refuel. As we were tying down our bird, the field and runway lights had gone off. Timing is everything! We then caught a taxi to an inexpensive motel ("cheap" doesn't sound right).

We had both been looking forward to crossing the famous and intriguing Mexican border into Juarez. But Bill's "Think I'll pass on the border crossing tonight, the sack sounds pretty good right now," summed up quite aptly how I felt, too. We both were some tired lieutenants.

We walked across the street and had a delicious *carne asada* for $1.45, which included flan, a custard-like dessert that was new to me. Bill said the name of the restaurant was "Llave Sus Manos", but I was sure he had misread the sign.

Next morning at five-thirty the sun was not quite up yet, but we were. Twenty minutes later, we were back in the ozone again, our departure having escaped the not-so-alert gaze of the El Paso tower personnel. In fact, no one on the field was aware that they had entertained two important flyers overnight.

Our next planned stop was Rodeo, New Mexico. There was some good news and some bad news. The good news was that we were finally out of Texas, but the other news was that there were some very ominous thunderstorms directly in our path. Since these clouds often contain severe turbulence, it was just common sense to divert around them, even if it meant returning to the point of departure.

By now we were flying at near our service ceiling, the highest altitude a plane can attain under normal conditions. In our case this was ranging between 5,000 and 5,500 feet above sea level. El Paso, where we had just taken off, was just under four thousand feet; Rodeo, our next landing point, was listed at 4,137 feet. This meant that even though we were reading five thousand feet on the altimeter, we were actually only a thousand feet above the terrain, when it was flat. The mountain ranges went on up from there.

"If those thunderstorms don't get us, those peaks will," Bill said cheerfully from the front seat. "That's the Continental Divide up ahead, you know."

I thanked him for his geographical expertise and pointed ahead to the towering granite located on both sides. Although lovely and picturesque, the formations had a distinct altitude advantage on us. We would be cutting it very close.

"Maybe we'd better circle around a couple of times and try to gain a little more height," I suggested. Bill nodded and began a gentle circling turn to the left. If the Little Clunker had any rivets, it would definitely be straining them now.

At 5,400 feet we began mushing through the air while the altimeter needle remained stuck in the same monotonous position.

"We could head south, Bill, into Mexico, but we don't have any maps for that area." Silence from Bill. As we flew up to the face of the mountain range, we could see automobiles slowly following the twisting highway that disappeared among the steep hills to the west.

"Well, Bill, do you want to go back to El Paso and buy a bigger plane? How about an automobile? We sure can't fly over these slopes, and to go around them has got to be too far."

"Then why not fly through them?" Bill answered. The same thought had been running through my mind.

He continued: "If we follow the highway—like, stay right above it, we'd at least be near some help if we needed it."

"What if the canyon turns out to be a box canyon?"

"Don't be crazy, Don. Box canyons only exist in Western movies. I'm for giving it a try." Neither of us even considered the possibility of encountering a tunnel. The man in front seemed pretty confident that the mail would go through, as it were. Strangely, an old aviation axiom flashed through my mind: "Never fly in the same cockpit with someone braver than you." Had I erred?

The mountains were around us now, looming up on both sides. The road, just a few feet below us, curved smoothly around its many turns. We were eyeball to eyeball with the motorists in their cars.

"Maybe we should lighten the ship by throwing out some luggage, like your spare tee-shirt," Bill suggested. This levity did not relieve the tension as we slowly passed a 1941 Chevrolet, exactly like the one my folks owned. Automobile identification is easy when you're only a few feet apart, and for a moment I thought I recognized the driver.

"Keep your eyes open for the summit elevation sign, Don. It had better be soon, 'cause we aren't going any higher, even if the road does." I was busy for the moment talking to the Box Canyon Gods.

"This has to be the longest canyon in the United States, but it's got to end somewhere."

"Probably back where we started," Bill replied, but for a change he was wrong. The canyon suddenly disappeared, revealing a staircase of descending hills and plateaus stretching off into the distance with the welcoming green fields of Tucson on the horizon.

"Do we live right, or what?" Bill exclaimed. I smiled knowingly and relaxed big-time, as we both settled back to enjoy the nice, three-thousand-foot glide into Tucson Airport.

We had a thick T-bone steak for brunch, since we had missed breakfast. After our repast, we entertained questions from the dozen or so people who came over to look at our Cub once the news of our big journey leaked out. The oil and dirt certainly gave the aircraft the appearance of having flown at least thirty thousand miles.

"Have any trouble?" someone asked.

"None to speak of," Bill said modestly. "Couple of precautionary landings but nothing we couldn't handle." I wondered to myself if he'd been on the same cross-country flight as I had, but, sensing his pilot's "Aw, it was nothing" attitude, I just smiled modestly.

"You boys will have to hustle if you intend to reach California tonight," the refueling pitman told us. "You'll probably run into some pretty strong headwinds through the pass at Beaumont-Banning."

"Yes, thank you. We do know a little about headwinds," I replied, although since the Florida episodes we had experienced tailwinds most of the way. The wind was extremely important, we were learning, in lightplane flying. In Corsairs, wind mattered only during the landing, and then only if it were a crosswind. Ironically enough, the F4U fighter could *taxi* faster than a Piper Cub could fly at its top speed.

"I'll take it as far as Blythe and you can have it from there," Bill offered. He knew I wanted to be at the helm when we landed in Claremont. It was important to impress the home folks.

After a quick stop for gas at Sky Harbor in Phoenix, we were under way again, almost on the final leg of our bodacious transcontinental dash. (Perhaps "saunter" would be more accurate.)

A sharp lookout was to be maintained, by my order, for the California State Line. Bill knew there was a distinct dividing line between Arizona and California, visible from the air, because I had told him so.

During the fifteen-minute refueling and comfort stop at Blythe, where the temperature was 107 degrees, we discovered a bad fabric rip on the topside of the right wing. To repair it would mean stopping for a patch job, which would take several hours. We both wanted to complete our journey, and the delay of another day was unacceptable. The pressure of the long cross-country trip was beginning to get to both of us.

Bill borrowed a pair of scissors and cut away the trailing strip of the offending fabric. This remedy seemed, at least temporarily, to solve the problem. The bad part of this solution was that any additional tearing along the upper surface of the wing could not be seen from either seat in the cockpit. We would need to land to inspect any further damage.

"I'm game if you are, Don. Let's launch. Maybe it's been that way since Jacksonville." We both knew that was not the case, but, in youthful exuberance, we took off anyway and headed for Banning Pass and, hopefully, Cable Claremont Airport.

As we passed Indio to the north of the Salton Sea, our ground speed was slowed to a mere trot. Thirty-five-mile-an-hour headwinds were upon us once again. Grazing cattle, had there been any, again would have had a slight speed advantage over the Cub. A desert dust storm reduced visibility to a joke, and we were forced to follow the highway at telephone pole height.

"We're not going to get around the corner at Banning," I informed Bill. He agreed. We landed at a dusty, windy Palm Springs Airport for more fuel. Bill wing-walked us to the gas pumps, as we could not stop the aircraft when the wind was from behind. The takeoff roll into this windstorm was all of 75 feet. Ten minutes later, we cleared the field boundaries.

After almost an hour, we turned left around the base of Mount San Jacinto and streaked toward Claremont at a breathtaking fifteen miles an hour, ground speed.

"I can't believe this, Bill. We're gonna need to refuel again, and we've only covered twenty-five miles. We don't want to arrive over Cable with a low fuel state *and* in the dark."

I then broke the news to him that I had never really seen Cable Airport except from the highway that paralleled it. Bill absorbed this new information unperturbed. We'd already agreed to another night landing, even though we both knew that the airport had not yet installed runway lighting.

At the Banning Airport we were able to locate someone who helped us top off fuel. I found a pay phone and called my folks, collect. My mother answered.

"Are you at the bus station, dear?"

"No, Mom, we're at the Banning Airport."

"You didn't hitchhike all that way, now did—?"

"No, Mom, we're flying in a small plane." Obviously, I had felt it unwise to trouble her ahead of time with the specifics of our mode of transportation.

"It'll be dark when we get there, so please have Dad drive out to Cable Airport. He can go right out on the runway; then have him back up the car all the way to the end of the runway, right up to the orange grove, facing west. Mom, west is toward Los Angeles."

"Right up to the orange grove," my mother repeated, clearly mystified.

"Yes, Mom, I'm sure he'll know which runway, there's only one. You'll hear us when we fly over in about an hour. We'll be coming right down Highway 66. When you hear us —no, you won't see us, our lights aren't working too well. When you hear us, have Dad flash the car lights on and off several times. Then we'll know it's clear, and you can put the lights on high beam. Please leave them on until we taxi back up the runway.

My mother repeated it back to me, just to make sure she had heard it right, but she did not sound convinced.

"Everything's fine, Mom, we do this all the time." Mothers sometimes worry.

After we took off from Banning, the wind died as suddenly as it had sprung up. We settled down to enjoy the scenic beauty of the famous highway below, even if it was too dark to see. I presumed that Bill had been in contact with the Wind Gods (assuming more than one to be on our case). I hoped he had also made up with whoever is in charge of aircraft fabric.

"There's Cucamonga, Bill. Those dark areas over there are vineyards, I'm pretty sure. This should be their harvesting season."

"How much farther?" Bill interrupted. He was apparently not interested in my little talk on viticulture. I told him we were almost there.

"Make sure your seat belt is fastened, and no smoking during the final approach to our destination, Claremont International." My spirits were visibly soaring as we neared our destination. We passed just south of the airfield, following the long string of car lights headed west on Route 66. Off to the right, in the center of a totally dark area, we could see a car's headlights blinking furiously.

"That's my dad, Bill, in the '41 Chevy Control Tower. This will be his first duty as an air traffic controller."

We circled the field at five hundred feet for an additional identification check and entered downwind. On our final approach we saw the car lights flick on to high beam. The soft squeal of the sausage tires on landing told us that the long voyage was over.

"No strain, Don. If it weren't so dark, your parents would have been proud of that landing."

As we taxied back up the runway, I could see my mother and father standing in the headlights. They had even brought my dog, Mongie. I cut the switches and extracted my tired body from the controls. My father was the nearest, and we shook hands warmly as my mother hurried over with a warm and welcome hug.

"Welcome home, dear. Did you have a nice flight?"

"Yes, Mom." What else could I say?

EPILOGUE

We kept the Cub at Cable Claremont for five months, giving our friends (mostly girls) personally guided airborne tours.

We then sold the Little Clunker for $600, gratefully pocketing the $120 profit.

Final and Official Summary
'37 Piper Cub Transcontinental Dash

Total statute miles flown:	3,100
Total hours flying time:	52
Average mph ground speed:	59.6
Days en route:	4

Expenses:

Aviation gasoline (including 14 gals. automobile gas)	$31.00
Oil, 5 qts. (not including two free 30-cent cans)	1.50
Pensacola BOQ lodging	0.00
Claridge Hotel, Houston ($3.50 each)	7.00
El Paso Motel ($4.00 each)	8.00
Meals and snacks	22.00
Damage to Bill's cordovan uniform shoes (est.)	10.00
Total trip cost:	$79.50
Actual cost per pilot:	$39.75

8 The Indestructible Dean

FIRST MET Dean Macho—his real name—in April of 1951 at Pohang Ni Dong, South Korea. The military called it simply K-3, which was a lot easier to pronounce. Dean was a quiet, soft-spoken pilot from North Dakota with brown eyes and a much-in-vogue crew-cut. He was a brand-new second lieutenant replacement pilot, having been commissioned less than six months earlier at Pensacola, Florida.

I remember seeing him in the adjutant's tent, checking into our Marine Corps fighter squadron, VMF-212. He was quite short, just under five foot nine, and I wondered if he would have trouble reaching the rudder pedals on our F4U-5 Corsairs. That sounds a little picky, I suppose, but not being able to apply full right rudder on takeoff to counter the powerful engine torque could be life-threatening.

Our airfield was located about ninety miles north of Pusan on the east coast of the peninsula. The base had one huge advantage in a world with very few navigation aids: distinctive landmarks. Returning from a combat hop in bad weather, the procedure was to head east, let down to the water, then

Two young second lieutenants, Dean Macho and James Shadrick, at K-3, the Pohang Ni Dong airfield, in the summer of 1951. *courtesy of Dean Macho*

fly south along the coast until we sighted a huge peninsula and bay jutting out beyond a nice white sandy beach. We turned right, landed, and were home. It was easily the best-loved bad-weather approach in all of Korea.

Dean was assigned to a different division from mine while he checked out in the new Corsairs. The new F4U-5 model was a bit more of a handful than the F4U-4 and -4B. It had three bombing pylons (versus two) and an automatic super-charger with a mind of its own that cut in during takeoffs, increasing the available power about 15 percent. We had lost the services of a replacement pilot, Second Lieutenant Jones, when his Corsair got away from him on takeoff and ground-looped right through a dozen parked aircraft and maintenance tents. Luckily, he missed everything, but his aircraft crashed and caught fire. Heroic measures from nearby marines pulled him from the inverted wreck, saving his life but at the cost of his left eye.

About one week later, in mid-April, Dean was assigned to fly on my wing as the Number Four man. Capt. Al Grasselli, an experienced, capable (and tall) pilot, was the division leader, with whom I had flown many times. Our combat mission went well from briefing to landing, although I was frustrated by Dean's wing position during the flight. He was so far aft that I could not have passed or received any visual signals if they had become necessary. I remember thinking that I had better square this new guy away or he would screw things up at some later date. First lieutenants sometimes get to thinking this way, particularly when they have second lieutenants on their wing.

We debriefed at Group Operations, after which I asked Dean to stop by my tent before the evening meal. He said he would, and we headed back to our respective sleeping areas.

I waited in our makeshift officers' club tent with a cold beer as company. About an hour later he shuffled in and ordered a beer but did not acknowledge my presence. Somewhat miffed, I went over and asked if he had forgotten my request to meet with me.

"No," he allowed; "I just haven't gotten around to it."

"Look, Macho," I began, "Your wing position today wasn't exactly conducive to good visual communications."

He set his beer down and put his hands on his hips. "So

what's with you?" He obviously had no respect for rank, or at least mine. I was losing my temper fast.

"I'm just trying to keep you on the right track. It's going to be a long war; and if you lost your radio . . . ."

He interrupted. "Hey, I don't think I need this crap! You're not my division leader, and I don't care if you've got fifty missions or whatever you've got."

I saw red. "Listen, you little shit. Your mouth's way too busy, and . . . ." I had said the maximally insulting word: not the expletive, but the *little*.

We both pushed some chairs out of the way and headed out the door. No one stopped us as we squared off, fists at the ready, Dean at his almost five feet, nine inches, 130 pounds; me at six feet, 160 pounds.

He moved in toward me, circling slightly. He was not bluffing, so I thought, *What the hell. I'll smack him a couple and we'll let this thing blow off.* Three quick left jabs to the side of my head, and I realized that this kid knew how to box. Now it was *my* mouth that had been too busy. As a small crowd gathered, as they always do in these cases, my first lieutenant's brain figured things out in a flash: Little guy versus bigger guy; little guy's a good boxer; bigger guy's in some trouble.

I did the only fair and sporting thing possible. I grabbed my opponent by his flight suit and fell on him. The extra thirty pounds served me well. After some insignificant and futile thrashing around, the onlookers pulled us apart and we combatants repaired to our respective corners to freshen up in our tents.

After dinner we met again in the officers' club. By then each of us had taken time to think things over a little. We both apologized, shook hands, and proceeded to get a little drunk together that evening. We became the best of friends later and continued the friendship for more than forty-six years. I never commented on his wing position again.

THE MISSIONS assigned to VMF-212 Squadron largely comprised two types: Armed Reconnaissance (the "armed reccy"), wherein the flight leaders located targets of opportunity and hit them accordingly; and the second and preferred mission, Close Air Support (CAS). The latter was always under the direct control of a Marine forward air controller, or FAC. A few other missions were controlled by airborne "Mosquito pilots," usually air force but sometimes army. They flew SNJ's (AT-6's) and would fly at treetop level to mark enemy targets with small smoke rockets. Everyone knew these guys all had a death wish, and their aircraft got hit by ground fire on almost every mission.

An armed reccy could be anything from boring to extremely interesting and usually was assigned to a section consisting of two aircraft, a more flexible and maneuverable unit than a four-plane division. A column of four aircraft, aside from being cumbersome, had a disadvantage when attacking a target: By the time the last man, "Tail-end Charlie," came by for his drop, the enemy gunners had the respective flight paths boresighted. Small wonder no one wanted to fly the Number Four slot.

The beauty of the two-place section tactic was that the following pilot had to keep track of only one aircraft, that flown by his leader, who, when a likely target was sighted, would announce something like: "Parked trucks dead ahead on the dirt road by the tree line. Use your twenties, etc." Both could strike in one pass.

Early in the Korean War it was common practice to circle around and make several runs. The Marine pilots, ever so quick to learn, figured out that the odds of being hit on that first pass were about 5 percent, while on the second and third passes the odds jumped to 85 to 90 percent. Like some income tax brackets, that seemed a high price to pay for opportunity.

Such laws of survival are relearned during every war. It became common knowledge that *one* pass was the only way to go if survival were to be a consideration. From this live-to-fight-another-day concept evolved a procedure that would not show up in historical or official accounts of fighter/ attack squadrons. It was called the "ready, fire, and aim" concept. Put another way, you took your best shot in the very few seconds allotted and got your ass out of there. It was not a matter of bravery or lack of guts, simply survival. The enemy gunners were not stupid, and shooting down a Marine Corsair that was making repeated strafing runs was a whole lot easier than trying to hit a plane that flew in and out, once, at somewhere near 350 miles an hour. If there was little or no enemy ground fire, the concept was usually not observed.

CAS missions under an FAC's directions were an entirely different matter, however. Usually four or even eight fighters were involved, and they were better suited to keep enemy gunners ducking for cover, as each aircraft would roll in on his firing run and cover for the pilot in front of him as he in turn expended his ordnance.

THAT PREAMBLE takes us to April 30, 1951, at K-3, South Korea. Second Lieutenant Macho by now had accumulated a grand total of six combat missions. He had flown over the so-called bomb line (a line carefully plotted daily, demarcating enemy and friendly positions) with several different pilots, but thus far he had not run into any significant enemy action. True, pilots could not be certain that they were being fired upon. The North Korean and Chinese ground troops rarely used tracer ammunition, so, unless an aircraft was actually hit, the pilot usually assumed that there was little or no enemy fire.

On this day Macho's mission was to fly wing on "Quiet" Eddie Torbett, a thin (and also tall) career marine captain. The two-plane section was to conduct an armed reccy north of the Choriwon Valley some fifteen to twenty miles above the bomb line. The ordnance load for each aircraft consisted of one belly drop-tank of 150 gallons, two napalm tanks, eight 5-inch HVARs (High Velocity Aircraft Rockets, equivalent to a 5-inch naval shell), and full 20-mm cannon rounds (for four guns).

After their briefing, which included information that the Chinese were assembling troops in an area adjacent to the Choriwon Valley, enemy antiaircraft fire (commonly referred to as "AA") had been reported by a previous flight as moderate. "Moderate," of course, covered everything from a lone soldier with a single-action .22 rifle to an antiaircraft battalion of quad fifties, along with five hundred angry enemy troops. Usually "light AA" meant that you didn't see any enemy fire, and "heavy AA" meant that they had actually hit your aircraft. When everything really went to hell and someone was shot down, the rating of the AA went up to "intense."

With favoring good weather, Captain Torbett set his course northward along the east coast of Korea for the approximate 150 miles to the bomb line. Turning inland at about the thirty-eighth parallel (which later would become very well known), the two Corsairs flew west toward the Choriwon Valley. Orbiting just to the north, the flight leader briefed his wingman.

"Blue Two, get in column and we'll make our runs from east to west with the sun behind us. I'll be pretty low—on the deck—so you stay five hundred feet above me. Keep me in sight. We'll pull out left. If there's anything real good, we may have to make a second pass. We'll drop napalm first. Save your rockets; if my napalm doesn't ignite, use your twenties to burn it. Check armament switches on. Any questions?"

There were none.

The leader eased power slightly and nosing over, headed down into the haze that had settled over the valley. Captain Torbett squinted through the reticles of his illuminated gun sight. A veteran of World War II and of some seventy-five missions in Korea, he was not far from completing his overseas tour and a return flight to his home in Arkansas.

"It looks like we've got some business here, Blue Two."

An acknowledgment clicked on the VHF radio. "Yeah, there's trucks, supplies, and a potfull of guys in quilted uniforms. Drop your napalm if you're in position. Do you have the targets in sight?"

"Negative, Blue Leader, just the general area, but I've got you in sight. I'll drop on your hits."

"That's a roger, Two. Man, there's a whole army down here."

Two liquid napalm tanks tumbled away from Torbett's aircraft and splashed along a small, winding dirt road. The expected fire mushroom did not materialize.

"Damn, they didn't light. Can you strafe it, Two?"

"Negative. I'm already past it. I do have the targets in sight now. You're right, they're everywhere."

"OK, Two, we'll have to make a second pass. I'll fire my rockets and twenties this pass, so I'll be a little higher. You can drop your napes and fire the twenties. Might help keep their heads down. I'm sure they're shooting at us, so fire-wall everything. We'll pull out to the south."

Another microphone click acknowledgment came from Blue Two, and both rolled in on a second firing pass. Macho could see his leader's rockets explode right in the middle of the target area. He rechecked his switches carefully and hoped he would do better on this pass, as he had overflown Torbett's napalm drop on the first one before he had been able to identify it. Unignited napalm is almost impossible to see from a cockpit any distance away.

"Blue One off, heading south. They're shooting at us, I guarantee!"

Macho wondered briefly how the captain could guarantee this, but he would sort that out later. He squeezed the trigger and four 20-mm cannon rocked the Corsair violently. He punched the red button next to the trigger, and the two napalm tanks separated and immediately splashed and exploded into one giant ball of fire. He had hit the center of the target area and briefly watched the burning crimson paths in his rearview mirrors.

He realized he was still firing his 20-mm guns, even though he had completed his run and was climbing out in a steep left-hand turn. Embarrassed, he quickly released the trigger and magically the guns ceased firing. As he turned in his seat to look for his leader, he felt a slight thud and then a huge BLAM! The Corsair staggered, and the smell of smoke filled the cockpit. The engine screamed in agony and then quietly sighed. He had been hit—but good.

"Blue Leader, I've taken some hits, losing power fast."

Glancing at the altimeter, Macho saw that he had twenty-five hundred feet. "I'm headed south, behind you. Do you have me in sight?"

"That's affirm. You're smoking pretty good. Do you have any fire in the cockpit?"

"Negative, just smoke, but no power at all now. The engine's had it."

"OK, Two; keep heading south toward our lines. You've got to bail out pretty soon or belly it in. The terrain is at about five hundred feet. I think I'd go over the side—pretty rocky down there, but it's your decision. I'll mayday your position and try to cover you."

"Roger, I'm going to jump. No place to put it in below."

So saying, Macho disconnected his radio cords and oxygen hose, cranked open the canopy, and dove over the left side of his crippled and done-for Corsair. He had completed the airborne portion of his seventh combat mission, except for the few feet remaining below him. His chute opened immediately, and he swung only twice before smacking down into a small rock-lined draw. He heard a muffled explosion and assumed that to be the death-cry of his beautiful former friend, the F4U-5 Corsair.

As he gathered his parachute around him, he saw his flight leader flash by, rocking his wings. He had been seen, and that was comforting. He knew Captain Torbett would climb for altitude and call for help. Macho also knew that the enemy would be looking for him. He wondered how far away they were and how far north of the front lines he was. He hid his chute behind some rocks and covered it with sand. He then checked his armament. He had his .38-caliber government-issue pistol, plus a small .32-caliber automatic that he always carried in the knee pocket of his flight suit. Satisfied that he was well armed for the coming events, 2d Lt. Dean Macho hunkered down to await his rescue—or capture. He contemplated his recent actions. Possibly his strafing and napalming of the approaching enemy troops might have made them a tiny bit angry.

Captain Torbett had done exactly what Macho imagined. He had spotted the downed pilot's chute on the ground and immediately climbed to five thousand feet and switched to Guard (emergency) Channel. He had relayed the ground coordinates and was pleased to learn that a navy helicopter happened to be airborne, on another mission, not too far south from the crash site.

"Can the chopper be diverted for a rescue mission?" Torbett had asked the control agency. "I've got a downed pilot very close to some enemy troops. I'm orbiting the site at five thousand."

"That's affirmative, Blue One. Remain this frequency. The chopper's call sign is Angel Seven." Several minutes later, the earphones in Torbett's helmet crackled.

"This is Angel Seven. Do you read, Blue One?"

"That's Roger, Angel Seven. What's your position?"

"We're about five miles south of the coordinates you gave. We're coming up the valley just below the Choriwon complex. Do you have the downed pilot's position in sight? We're familiar with that valley. We've attempted two extractions [rescues] this week. The area is loaded with enemy troops. Couldn't get either of the pilots out."

"Roger, Angel Seven, I'm still at five thousand. I think I have you visually. I don't have the pilot in sight, but I know which canyon he's holed up in. I'll drop down and fly right above his position. When I'm directly over the site, I'll fire my twenties. You should see the smoke, and maybe it'll slow down the enemy troops a little. They're only a few hundred yards from the downed pilot now."

"Roger, Blue One. We'll only be able to make one pass. Hope you understand that."

Captain Torbett knew only too well the HO3S Sikorsky helicopter's vulnerability to ground fire. He hoped Macho would realize that the chopper could not land and that he would have only one quick moment to grab the rope ladder dangling below the helicopter. The rescue equipment in 1950–51 was very basic, with no hydraulic hoists or rescue baskets.

Blue Leader rolled into his strafing and marking run, hoping for the best. As he flew by Macho's position, he opened up with all four 20-mm cannon. Bullets and rocks exploded in every direction. He pulled up sharply and turned to make a second run, only this time he would not be firing. He figured the enemy would not know this.

The two-man rescue helicopter entered the small canyon following a dried-up streambed. As they rounded a slight bend, the pilot and his crewman beheld a scene right out of a cheap Western movie. Standing in the center of the streambed was someone in a flight suit, wearing a large gold helmet and firing both pistols at something further up the canyon.

"If that's not John Wayne, then he's got to be the guy we're looking for," the chopper pilot informed his crewman on the intercom.

The helicopter flared to a brief hover; Macho turned, and, after one final parting shot, grabbed the rope ladder with a death grip. He had heard the welcome sound of the rotor blades and—as Torbett had hoped—realized that, in these unfriendly surroundings, he had but one chance to get aboard the rescue chopper.

The crewman had to pry the pistols from Macho's hands, as they were inadvertently pointed upward toward the helicopter. The Angel Seven pilot wheeled the helicopter around sharply, pulled up the collective and twisted the throttle to the red line, and, as the phrase goes, hauled ass out of there.

Once safely over the front lines, Macho crawled forward in the narrow helicopter cabin and gave the pilot a grateful pat on the shoulders, which was acknowledged by a broad smile. The three occupants then settled down for the thirty-minute ride to the warmth and comfort of the air force base at Suwon (K-13).

The next morning, May 1, after a convivial evening with his new air force friends in their club, where Macho was toasted and hailed as a real gun-totin' Marine, he was returned to K-3 and his squadron mates. "Two-gun" Macho had finally completed Combat Mission Number Seven.

Dean was understandably the center of attention at the squadron "O" club that evening. His narrow-escape story was told and retold to an appreciative and understanding audience. Captain Torbett also received well-deserved congratulations for excellent coordination and downed-pilot coverage —excellence that did not go unnoticed by the rescued pilot, either.

In VMF-212 it was an unwritten tradition that any pilot who had been shot down and was lucky enough to be rescued would be offered a week's R&R in Japan, if he so desired. Macho, seemingly unflappable, disdained to accept this recuperative rest leave and instead asked to be placed on the flight schedule for the following day.

ON 2 MAY 1951, Second Lieutenant Macho duly appeared, ready to fly. The mission: Capt. Al Grasselli would lead a flight of four Corsairs on an assigned CAS mission. They would be working directly with a Marine FAC who would be guiding the flight in to help support a Marine battalion that reportedly was surrounded and badly outnumbered.

The flight briefed, taxied out, and took off to the west, past the famous OOPS sign someone had facetiously placed at the very end of the elevated runway. Once airborne, the division wheeled north for the forty-minute run to the bomb line and the required check-in with Devastate Baker, the direct air support center, which would then pass them on to their controller.

How appropriate, thought Macho. *I wonder who dreams up these call signs.*

His position in the flight was as Number Two man on the flight leader's right wing. The second section was led by Capt. Joe Dehaven, a popular squadron member from Boston, and on his wing was 1st Lt. Dock Pegues. Dock had been with the squadron since its departure from the United States and was known for his Southern accent, good wing position, and keen sense of humor. He, too, was a veteran of World War II.

Dean had been watching his instruments more than casually thus far on the mission, as the oil temperature gauge showed a slightly higher than normal reading. Conversely the oil pressure was slowly dropping—not rapidly, but steadily. He hated to announce this information to the flight leader, as it was not yet bad enough to warrant turning back. On the other hand, they would be checking into the control agency in a few minutes and then be directed into enemy territory.

"Black Leader, this is Two. My oil pressure is running a little low, right around sixty PSI. The oil temp is up slightly, too."

"Roger, Two, do you wish to return to base?" *What a rotten question.* Macho knew that if he left the formation, he would be assigned an escorting wingman, reducing the flight's strength to only two aircraft.

"Well, I'd like to continue and see if it will settle down."

Macho knew he sounded unsure of himself, but he had never been in this grey area of decision making before. He knew how humiliating it would be to bring an aircraft back with some sort of engine trouble and then have the maintenance people not find anything wrong. Yes, he would continue the flight.

"OK, Two, keep me posted. Flight, go to channel six for check-in with Devastate Baker."

As Grasselli rattled off his division's total ordnance loads,

Macho kept his eyes glued on the engine instruments. The cylinder-head temperature began moving up steadily, and opening the cowl flaps for cooling had not helped.

"What a God-damned quandary," he thought. "I hate to be a quitter, but this thing is starting to run pretty hot." Suddenly, his mind was made up for him. The engine had started to run rough. It wasn't missing, but it was enough to crystallize his thinking.

"Black Leader, let's go tactical." All four pilots shifted their radio frequencies.

"This is BlackTwo, engine's running rough. Everything is runnin' too hot."

"OK, Black Flight." Grasselli's voice came through as calm as if he were discussing the weather back home. In two wars he had seen a lot of action. "Black Three, escort Two home. I'd suggest a route via Kangnung that we just passed over. It's in friendly hands, but I think the strip is only about fifteen hundred feet usable."

"Roger from Black Three. I'll join on you, Two. Let's try to hold seven thousand feet if we can." Black Two thumbed the mike in acknowledgment and turned quickly to the south and home base.

"Good luck, Two. Black Four, it's you and me now; let's go channel three."

Macho checked his instruments carefully as Black Three joined on his wing. They remained on their tactical frequency.

"Black Three, from Two. I can't maintain altitude, engine's running rougher by the minute. I don't think we can make it back to K-3. The engine feels like it might have swallowed a piston."

Silence took over as the two Corsairs headed south. Kangnung was a newly acquired, mostly dirt strip and used mainly as a forward area airfield for small liaison and observation light aircraft. It had no tower and no fire-fighting or crash equipment, but it had one huge attribute: It was close by.

"I think I'm committed to Kangnung," Macho transmitted. "But I've no idea where it is exactly." His seven missions had not been enough to have thoroughly acquainted him with the terrain and emergency fields.

"Not to worry, Two; I've flown over it a bunch of times. Liberty is not too good, but I hear the C rations are quite tasty."

The attempt at humor by his escort was lost on Macho, who had his hands full with a crippled Corsair that—once again—probably would not get him home. His altimeter read forty-five hundred feet as they descended slowly.

"I've got Kangnung in sight, Black Two. It's at one o'clock right beside that dry riverbed. We've got plenty of altitude, so you should be able to put it down there. Do you see the strip?"

"Roger, I see the riverbed but not the strip. Is the strip parallel to the river?" A pause, and then the sixty-four-dollar question: "What do you think about the gear?" Macho was asking for an opinion as to landing wheels-up or -down.

"It's up to you. The strip's under two thousand feet long. I'm not really sure exactly. Everything would have to be perfect to set it down on the end and get it stopped. You probably don't have enough power for a go-around, so you'll be on a one-time approach."

It was good advice, Macho knew. He would have to put it in right on the money. He hated to smash up another airplane, but his instinct for self-preservation overrode the prospect of bending the aircraft. He had not made any decisions yet, except that he wanted to walk away from his upcoming landing.

He heard himself say, "Black Three, I'm going to leave the

gear up and use thirty degrees of flaps. I think that's my best chance. The strip looks too short to get in. The riverbed looks a ton better. Here I go!"

Black Three did not offer any further advice. He had done everything he could to help out his wingman. It was always left up to the pilot with the emergency to make his own decisions, right or wrong. It *was* his ass on the bottom line.

Black Three poured on the power and dove rapidly on ahead, screaming down the short airstrip. He hoped all hands would be alerted that something unexpected was going to happen.

Macho gauged his altitude carefully, along with his airspeed. He locked open the canopy, cranked down partial flaps, and checked again that the landing gear handle was up—not a normal feeling. With a final tightening of his shoulder straps, he leveled his wings, flying toward the center of the streambed. He held the Corsair in a three-point attitude and hoped. Almost gently the aircraft touched down onto the sand, its four-bladed propeller suddenly bent backward, acting as both a huge plough and a brake. The Corsair skidded ahead in a straight line, finally coming to a stop as it skewed 90 degrees to the left. No fire, just a lot of riverbed dust.

Macho shut off all the switches, undid his shoulder straps, lap belt, and radio cords and hastily climbed down out of the aircraft. He saw his wingman fly by, this time slowly, and waved that he was safe. Black Three waggled his wings in acknowledgment and headed for the barn.

In a minute or two a Marine jeep appeared with a sergeant behind the wheel. He stared first at the Corsair sitting despondently in the riverbed and then somewhat quizzically at the aviator standing before him. The mutual stare-down ended when Macho spoke:

"Hello, Sergeant. So . . . what's the movie for tonight?"

LIFE TENDS at times to settle into routines, sometimes unusual routines. Macho gets shot down. Macho comes home in a small plane. Macho is the honored guest speaker at happy hour in the "O" club. Macho disdains to accept the relaxing R&R trip to nearby Japan. Displaying steelly nerves, Macho asks the flight scheduling officer to place his name on the flying list for the morrow.

The returning warrior has also predicted to his two tentmates, second lieutenants Beers and Ballmer, also brandnew replacement pilots, that any day now he, just like the other marine pilots in the squadron, would be returning his assigned aircraft to its rightful parking spot on the flight line, *and* his aircraft would be undamaged, in good flying condition.

ON 4 MAY 1951, Capt. Eddie Torbett, Dean's favorite rescue coordinator, informed him that he, Dean, had been assigned to fly in another division and that this was done at the order of the commanding officer, Lt. Col. Claude Welch. The reason given was, quote, "For a change of luck."

The afternoon mission was another CAS mission, and his new division leader was Capt. Jack Wilkinson, a veteran fighter pilot who had completed more than sixty missions in Korea. The captain was also five-foot-nine, with a ready smile and a quiet disposition. He was nearing the end of his overseas tour and was known to be a careful but aggressive pilot. His section leader was Capt. Bob Stigall, a reserve officer from St. Joseph, Missouri, who was easily the best poker player in the squadron. His sharp blue eyes never missed a thing. Bringing up the rear as "Tail-end Charlie" was another replacement pilot, 2nd Lt. J. J. Prior. On only his third combat mission, Prior was already popular with the other pilots. His ready smile and good looks matched his good nature. (Lt. Prior

Ten fighter pilots, ready for combat, pose in front of an F4U-5 Corsair at K-3. Macho (*kneeling*) is in the center. *courtesy of Dean Macho*

would be killed a few weeks later in bad weather conditions; South Korean farmers found him, still strapped in his seat, in his smashed Corsair.)

The weather was marginal in the target area at briefing time, so the mission was put on hold. The crews had to just sit around and wait—always the hardest part of combat flying. Dean learned that both captains had completed South Pacific combat tours in World War II. Captain Stigall had shot down several Japanese aircraft and had another two listed as "probables."

Finally, the weather was reported to be clearing in the target area, and individual instrument departures were to be conducted, with tops estimated at seven to eight thousand feet. As the flight taxied out past the OOPS sign, Gold Four inadvertently taxied over a 20-mm ammo link and was forced to return to the line for a tire change or a replacement aircraft. There were none, so Gold Flight numbered only three fighters: Captain Wilkinson leading, Captain Stigall, and Lieutenant Macho.

Gold Flight rendezvoused on top at seventy-five hundred feet, formed a loose three-plane "V," and headed north to deal with the enemy however they could. A solid undercast shielded their expected target area, they learned when they checked in with the Direct Air Support Center. The flight was then assigned an alternate target and given a check-in radio frequency and the call sign of a Mosquito spotter aircraft already airborne.

This ought to be exciting, thought Macho. It would be his first experience with one of the daredevil spotters. He checked the announced target coordinates, and they seemed familiar. As they flew westward, the weather improved rapidly to only a few layers of scattered clouds.

"Mosquito Dash Five, this is Gold Leader, a flight of three F4U-5s." Wilkinson rattled off their combined ordnance and was told by the Mosquito to descend to sixty-five hundred feet in a left-hand orbit.

"The target consists of many troops, mostly dug in, but some right out in the open. Believe me, they're here in industrial strength! Looks like they're in some sort of a staging area. I'll mark the target with a white smoke rocket. Understand you have two 500-pounders and eight rockets each aircraft. Suggest you drop the five hundreds first and then the rockets along with the 20-millimeters. I wouldn't get too low; the AA is very accurate. I relieved Mosquito Four and he got hit several times, but he made it home. I'll be orbiting to the west."

"Roger from Gold Leader. We'll make our runs from north to south on your smoke."

As the three Corsairs circled safely at altitude awaiting the Mosquitos' actions, Macho felt a slight chill. They were over the Choriwon valley, the scene of his earlier narrow escape.

"Tally-ho, Mosquito Five. Got your smoke in sight. Let's go, boys! Check armament switches on."

Gold Leader rolled in to a modified bomb run, as it was customary to begin such runs from a higher altitude. He pickled off both bombs and pulled out at the pre-briefed altitude of three thousand feet. This altitude would prevent the flight members from flying into their own bomb blasts and minimize the enemy's antiaircraft effectiveness. They would then fire their rockets and 20-mm guns on the second and final run.

Macho lined up his target through the illuminated gun sight and punched the bomb-release button. Pulling back sharply on the stick, he climbed back up to altitude and switched the armament switches from bombs to rockets. He noticed the target was covered with dirt, dust, and grey-black smoke, the latter resulting from the 500-pounders.

"Good runs, Gold Flight. You're right on target. There are some trucks and supplies about a half a mile south of your last target. If you can hit those targets, we could call it a day."

"That's a roger, Mosquito Five. Flight, follow me in with your rockets and guns. We'll have to pull out lower this time, so we'll make a running rendezvous to the south."

In his rocket run, Macho concentrated on locating the leader's hits. "One more run," he thought, "and we'll be out of here." He had not seen any ground fire, but he knew that it was very hard to see unless tracer ammunition were being used. His hits were right on target next to the leader's.

Satisfied with his day's work, Macho safetied his armament switches and banked slightly to the left as he climbed out from the target area.

A big bang ruined his warm feeling. The aircraft started to roll violently, and he could see pieces flying off his left wing. He had been hit with something big, possibly a 37-mm projectile. Full right stick leveled the aircraft momentarily.

"This is Gold Two. I'm hit! Left wing—can't hold it straight and level. I may have to leave this thing." The altimeter read seventeen hundred feet, and he knew he was only about a thousand feet above the ground.

"Roger, Two. Keep heading south. What's your altitude?"

"Fifteen hundred feet. I'm headed south, but I don't think I can hold the left wing up. I've got power but I'm losing control. I can see the ground through the hole in the wing."

"OK, Two, jump if you have to. We'll cover you."

At that instant Macho realized that the aircraft was on the verge of becoming uncontrollable. He knew he needed about nine hundred feet of altitude to clear the aircraft and for the chute to open. There was no time to disconnect anything. He cranked open the canopy; as he released the safety belt, he was immediately thrown from the cockpit. He was tumbling wildly and for a brief moment thought about trying to stop the unwanted somersaults. Remembering his proximity to the ground, he yanked the parachute D ring mightily. It opened with a gut-wrenching jerk. He swung to and fro briefly and then smacked into a soft sandy area. The landing site looked strangely familiar.

Up above, rescue efforts were under way. Captain Wilkinson ordered Gold Three, Captain Stigall, to climb for altitude and put out a Mayday. Gold Leader had not been able to locate the downed pilot, although he had returned to the target area and circled, frantically searching for Macho's position. It was imperative to find him before the enemy did.

The treatment he could expect from soldiers who had just been bombed, rocketed, and strafed was not a pretty thought. Wilkinson did not know for sure whether Dean had even survived the bailout. In the 1950s, pilot survival radios were not part of the standard equipment.

Gold Three reported that a rescue chopper was on the way to their coordinates. He also noted that it was 4:30 in the afternoon—only a couple of hours till darkness. After that, they all knew the downed pilot would have no chance of being rescued.

The orbiting Corsairs were taking turns squirting off a few rounds of their remaining 20-mm ammunition as a deterrent to the searching enemy troops. The black smoke marking where Macho's plane had crashed and exploded could be seen for miles.

"This is Angel Three Zero approaching from the south. Where is the downed pilot in relation to the black smoke? What is your position, Gold One?"

"Roger from Gold One. We're about a mile west of the smoke at thirty-five hundred feet. We do not have the pilot in sight. Neither of us saw him bail out." There followed a few minutes of silence while the chopper pilot thought about this.

"I'll make a couple of runs into the area, but we can't survive if there's very much AA."

"Roger that," from Gold One. "I'd guess he's in one of those small canyons, but I don't know which one. Perhaps you should . . . ."

"Stand by, Gold Leader. My crewman just spotted a signal mirror flashing. I hope that's our guy."

The two Marine pilots were now circling the helicopter, ready to provide covering fire should it become necessary. As the rescue helicopter flew toward the flashing mirror, the helicopter pilot spoke on the intercom to his crewman: "Charlie, somehow this place looks familiar."

The chopper pilot's déjà vu must have made his head spin, for just ahead in the middle of a small, narrow canyon stood a flight-suited pilot wearing a large gold crash helmet. This pilot, too, was out of Central Casting for a Western movie, as he was holding a pistol in each hand, apparently ready to deal with any and all bad men.

The rope-ladder trick was repeated as the helicopter swooped down into the streambed area, flaring as it had when they rescued a Marine pilot five days before. Once the downed pilot was safely climbing up the rope ladder, the chopper beat a hasty retreat southward, now with three souls on board, just like the last time.

"Jesus Christ, it's Macho!" the helicopter pilot exclaimed when he had a moment to look back at the rescuee. The same canyon, the same two-gun pilot—the coincidences were almost unimaginable.

Dean and the chopper pilot had gotten somewhat acquainted on their earlier ride together back to K-13. Macho had told him about the entire mission and how he had been hit by ground fire farther north in the Choriwon Valley. It was the same story all over again. And, once again, both pilots agreed: Macho was indeed a lucky son-of-a-gun.

Mission Number Nine was now in the books, but the coincidences kept piling up. The same navy liaison pilot had flown Dean back to his base at K-3. Macho had bailed out and landed almost exactly where he had landed a few days before. The same helicopter crew had pulled him out from nearly certain capture and possible death. He had even used the same rope ladder.

Luck aside, another item bothered Macho a lot: He had lost three aircraft in a row! His two tent-mates callously pointed out that, with just two more such losses, he would become a North Korean ace.

But another big night was celebrated by all the pilots in the "'O" club tent. Dean by now was well on the road to becoming a polished public speaker. His demeanor, illuminated by his apparent invincibility, bordered on the self-assurance of the mentally unbalanced. His good luck at being rescued definitely overshadowed the bad luck of being shot down.

Lt. Col. Welch, a wise and considerate commanding officer, removed Dean from his seat on the edge of immortality by again bringing up the magical and recuperative powers of an R&R in Japan. Dean allowed that this plan had merit and accepted it with quiet graciousness. Although he now felt indeed indestructible, he decided not to push his luck any further.

EPILOGUE

Second Lt. Dean Macho completed eighty-nine combat missions in Korea without damaging any more U.S. aircraft. Interestingly, while on a later R&R visit to Japan, by accident he ran into the helicopter pilot who had twice saved his life. The two pilots became good friends and corresponded regularly for many years.

Dean outlasted his tent-mates, second lieutenants Beers and Ballmer, who were both killed a little later flying combat missions in Korea. Had they survived, they might have enjoyed kidding Dean, who later *did* become a "North Korean ace." Upon returning to the United States, while assigned to a squadron in Quantico, Virginia, Dean had to bail out after an engine failure—yes, in a Corsair—and had to belly-in another during an FCLP (Field Carrier Landing Practice) flight, just short of the runway. Both Corsairs received "A" (strike, i.e., total) damage; and with these two crashes, he brought his score up to a verifiable five. Fortunately for him, none were attributed to pilot error.

Dean had a very successful Marine Corps career, retiring as a colonel in June 1975 after twenty-six years of service. His indestructibility expired on 27 July 1997, when he made his final landing, a heart attack victim. A brave fighter and a true friend, he turned out to be more than tall enough. I miss him.

9 The Ripcord, MacSweeny

NICKNAMES ARE an interesting phenomenon. Some are complimentary, like "Lucky Lindy," and some tell stories, like "Wrong Way" Corrigan. Still others allude to physical characteristics: "Potato Chin" Curtis, for example, and "Shay Al," he with a slight lisp. These monikers are usually indelibly affixed on the spur of the moment. Such was the case of "Iwo Jima" MacSweeny.

Aviation Cadet John MacSweeny was an average guy, to be sure. He was from a small town in Ohio, about five foot nine, a little pudgy, with a slightly receding hairline. Not quite handsome, he had sparkling blue eyes and was about two years older than most of the other cadets.

All of the naval cadets were in some stage of the U.S. Navy's Primary Flight Training Program at the Naval Air Station, Memphis, Tennessee. The members of class 14B, of which MacSweeny was one, were awaiting their turns to begin actual flight training in the famed N2S Stearman. This open-cockpit biplane served both the Army Air Corps and the U.S. Navy as their primary flight trainer. Nicknamed the "Yellow

Peril," this extremely hard-to-land airplane had washed out many a cadet. It was the winter of 1946, and the war in the Pacific had ended some four months before.

Cadets in those days, like Annapolis midshipmen, were not allowed overnight liberty, wives, cars, or civilian clothes —not really much of anything. Attending the nightly movie inevitably became a ritual. Even if you hated movies, you went. It filled the 7:00-to-9:00 p.m. void nicely, leaving only an hour before lights out. Good movies were as scarce as girls.

On one particular evening MacSweeny and his closer friends (the inner group of cadets of 14B fame) had just finished viewing for the third time the epic *Sands of Iwo Jima,* starring John Wayne. After the brass had been cleared and the artillery smoke had lifted, the cadets were returning to their respective barracks when MacSweeny turned to one of his buddies and said, facetiously:

"Boy, it was a lot tougher on that island when I was there."

This remark was overheard by others not in MacSweeny's group. Since MacSweeny looked older, acted older, and was an unassuming kind of guy, it was immediately apparent that he must have served on Iwo Jima: hence the nom de plume, "Iwo," for short. Naturally, when questioned about his island tour of duty, MacSweeny always demurred, saying something like, "I'd prefer not to talk about it." He was always careful never to state outright that he had *ever* been to Iwo Jima. In truth, his longest journey from home had been to visit an aunt in Cleveland, not far from his home in Akron, Ohio.

Cadets always operated as a group apart. They trained, played, and flew as a separate class of beings. The officers did not associate with them because they were not officers, and the enlisted ranks only tolerated them because they would *become* officers. Consequently, prestige in the clannish cadet world was a highly coveted commodity that essentially

Cadet Tooker (*facing camera*) chats with the legendary "Iwo Jima" MacSweeny at NAS Memphis in 1946. This is the only known photograph of MacSweeny.

amounted to peer recognition. Even negative prestige or notoriety was better than no recognition at all.

A cadet in an earlier class, for example, who had ground-looped his Stearman twice, was a celebrity. Another guy in the same class bragged that he was valedictorian of his summer school in Missoula, Montana. Anything that made a cadet different or made him stand out was of great prestigious value. Hence, Cadet John MacSweeny enjoyed a certain measure of distinction, albeit ill gotten.

The cadets of 14B were extremely anxious to begin actual flying, MacSweeny particularly so. On a rare visit to downtown Memphis he had purchased a forlorn, well-worn white silk scarf from the Goodwill store for fifty cents. A white scarf had always been the trademark of an aviator, and with open cockpit flying it was a very practical article for the pilots. However, the cadet clan had standards for scarves. No one wanted to be seen wearing a shiny, brand-new scarf. It also must be reported that MacSweeny had a white knitted woolen scarf that his mother had thoughtfully sent him, neatly folded in the bottom of his footlocker. This other scarf never saw the light of day.

The cadets of 14B ultimately completed ground school, ending eight hours a day of navigation, aerodynamics, power plants, aerology, code, blinker, and physical conditioning. The daily sight and sound of the yellow trainer aircraft overhead gave them more than enough incentive for the hard work needed to pass all of the ground-school subjects. Now the prospect of finally taking off, climbing into the skies, and taking over the controls was constantly on MacSweeny's mind. However, he could not have imagined what lay in store for him.

Dawn broke on a cold but clear January morning. It had snowed over the weekend, and patches of snow still lingered on the ground. Those students of class 14B lucky enough to have an instructor assigned to them along with an aircraft were to begin their familiarization flights ("A" stage). Instructors and aircraft were always in short supply. Nevertheless, all cadets had to be ready for flying regardless of instructor or aircraft availability. By 7:30 a.m. MacSweeny had been fitted for his parachute at the paraloft and had put on his winter flying jacket and fleece-lined boots over his uniform shoes. He declined to wear the heavy winter pants because they were too bulky; very few of the pilots wore them. He was ready.

Finally, there was his name on the schedules board, right under that of his newly assigned instructor. It read: "Mac-Carthy—MacSweeny A-1." There was even an aircraft number following that, which meant only one thing: The mission was a go!

At five minutes to nine he heard what he had been waiting

almost two years to hear: "MacSweeny?" someone called out. The instructor raised his arm and then extended his hand. He smiled as his cadet approached.

"Cadet MacSweeny reporting, Sir." They shook hands.

"OK, MacSweeny, I see you've got all your gear. Does your chute feel comfortable? You have gloves? It'll be cold up there."

"Yes, Sir, the chute feels fine." He then produced his leather gloves to show to the instructor.

"Good, I'll meet you at the plane and we'll go over the aircraft preflight inspection together. Do you have any questions?"

"No, Sir, I'll meet you at the aircraft."

"All right, I'm going to finish my coffee and then I'll be right out."

MacSweeny walked out to the flight line and to his "Yellow Peril" with his excitement barely contained. He could feel his parachute bumping him from behind with each step. His mind processed many thoughts as he carefully sidestepped the puddles still standing on the concrete apron. He had not noticed his instructor's rank; all he knew was that his name was MacCarthy.

That's a break, he thought, *maybe we're both Scots.*

The instructor's arrival interrupted his reflections. He noted that MacCarthy was dressed in the same bulky winter flying jacket, leather helmet, and boots with the fleece lining. The instructor was also wearing a white scarf.

"All right, MacSweeny, we'll walk around the ship together and look for anything unusual, any rips, tears, broken wires, et cetera. Be sure and always check the underside of both wing tips. You never know. If the guy before you gets a wing tip and doesn't report it, and you fail to spot it, you'll be blamed."

"Yes, Sir," was all that he could manage.

"OK, MacSweeny, you can help the plane captain there crank her up. When she's going good, jump in the back seat and I'll engage the starter."

The venerable hand crank would not be replaced by the electric starter for a number of years and was still putting more blisters on cadets' hands than the parallel bars at the gym. In fact, washed-out cadets were often assigned to the flight line while awaiting transfer orders so that they could help start their successful buddies' planes. This was perhaps cruel and unjust, but then sitting on a bunk and sobbing into one's now irrelevant white scarf served no useful purpose.

MacSweeny shared the cranking of the inertia starter and then jumped into the rear cockpit. The engine roared into life as he refastened his parachute harness and checked his safety belt. He then connected the two plastic Gosport tubes that ran from the instructor's mouthpiece back to the earphones in his leather helmet. The instructor did all the talking, the cadet all the listening. This arbitrary system could be somewhat frustrating to the student, but it was effective.

"You all set?" the instructor asked.

MacSweeny's lips formed the words, "Yes, I am." The mirrors on the upper wing just in front of the instructor's head allowed him to look up and see the student in the rear seat.

"I'll taxi out, then we'll check the mags and take off. Is this your first time up?"

MacSweeny nodded in the affirmative. It was the first time he had even sat in any airplane. He noticed that he could see the instructor's eyes through his goggles in the mirror whenever he looked back at him. They were warm and friendly, as was his voice. This was not going to be so difficult after all.

The engine checked out perfectly, and a green light from the tower signified permission to take off. The Stearmans were not radio equipped. A turn into the wind, a short run, and they were airborne.

"How do you like it, Mac?"

Again the nod, as their eyes met in one of the small mirrors.

"I'll climb her up to about four thousand and we'll just take a look around. I want you to learn our landmarks. That's the City of Memphis over there on your left. The Naval Air Station, called "Mainside," is just behind us now. Out ahead is your main navigational aid, which we call the Mississippi River."

Everything looked like a mosaic, with toy cars, small square fields, and miniature houses displayed below. The wind in MacSweeny's face, the sound of the engine, and the singing of the wire rigging were even better than he had imagined. He tucked his tattered scarf in a little further under his warm fur-lined collar.

"How do you feel, Mac, OK? Sometimes some of the students get a little queasy on their first ride."

MacSweeny nodded again that he was feeling just fine and that the ride was great. The thought of having to explain airsickness—in a purported combat veteran!—was too bitter to even contemplate.

"I'll do a few turns and banks and throw it around a bit just to let you get the feel of maneuvering. Then you can take the controls and get the hang of it yourself."

MacSweeny decided right then and there that he would cut his wrists and fall on his sword for good measure before he would admit to any kind of airsickness. He gave the instructor a double thumbs-up, which could only mean, "I'm game for anything, Sir!"

"Good, I like to see someone who really likes to fly. Me, I still love it and guess I always will. Say, would you like to see some mild acrobatics? Nothing violent, of course."

MacSweeny's "Let's give it a go," was lost in the slipstream.

"OK, double-check your safety belt and we'll start with a slow roll to the left. All set? Here we go!"

MacSweeny put both hands on the left side of the cockpit to hold on. As the plane continued its rolling motion to the left, he decided to improve his grip by moving both hands to the right side. He let go and reached across the cockpit for better support. All he got was air! Suddenly "Iwo Jima" Mac-Sweeny was alone in space, without an airplane.

The strange new quietness and the reality of what had just happened could not penetrate the fog of his disbelief. He reached around himself gingerly for the airplane. It simply was not there, no matter where he reached. Finally, he spotted it—tiny in size and far above him, framed against the blue sky.

He could hear his own voice clearly: "Where's my airplane going without me?"

Looking down, he could see the ground still in miniature but getting larger by the second. It was obvious that he was falling, although he felt no particular sensation of falling. He was turning over slowly, but he had not the vaguest notion of how to control his descent.

As for figuring out how and why he had suddenly left the airplane, that would have to wait. There was another, more pressing problem at hand.

Never having actually opened a parachute, MacSweeny, even in his dazed condition, definitely remembered that the magic word was *ripcord*. "The ripcord, MacSweeny—the ripcord!" he reminded himself. (High overhead, his appalled instructor was saying more or less the same thing, because he hadn't seen a parachute bloom yet and it was past time.) Now where, exactly, was the ripcord? It was that D-shaped handle, he knew that much.

A search for the ripcord revealed it to be on the left side and not on the right. The ground suddenly was not in miniature anymore; it was now in full living color. *I'd best get this chute opened soon or there'll be no movie for me tonight,* he realized. *Give a yank! Those high-tension lines sure look close, and you wouldn't want to. . . .*

BLOP! MacSweeny plunged vertically into a muddy snowdrift like a 16-pound shot into a vat of peanut butter. He was in up to his goggles. As his parachute settled around him, somewhere Lady Luck wiped the nervous perspiration from her brow.

Meanwhile, a yellow biplane droned above. In the front cockpit sat a totally distraught and shaken instructor. He had just killed his student! He had felt and seen MacSweeny leave the aircraft and had been able to follow his downward plunge for ten to fifteen seconds. It had seemed to be an eternity while waiting for the sight of a blossoming parachute. But alas, no chute, only a speck growing smaller and smaller, finally disappearing from his view entirely.

Heartsick, he had throttled back and dived toward the general area, circling for a closer look. Nothing. No chute, no activity of any kind. Several low passes over the area only confirmed what he knew must be the terrible truth. The boy had frozen from fear and had failed to open his chute. Grief-stricken but resolute, MacCarthy opened the throttle wide and headed for home base to report the tragedy.

Below, for several minutes MacSweeny stood motionless. He was implanted in mud underneath a snowdrift. At first he thought he was dead, then alive but blind. Removing the snow from his goggles solved the blindness problem. As he completed his personal body inventory, it became apparent that no bones were broken, either. He had looked up at the N2S and seen only one head silhouetted in the front cockpit as it flew by, quite low. He had waved both arms, sure that he could be seen even from his snowy foxhole. The plane had continued circling for about five minutes and had then departed to the east. He guessed that his instructor had seen him and was going for help.

Looking around at his new home, MacSweeny observed with interest that he had come down exactly between two parallel rows of high-tension lines. A few feet to either side and he would have been fried like a bug on an electric insect eradicator.

I must weigh three hundred pounds with all this flying gear, snow, and mud. He smiled to himself as the phrase, "ol' stick-in-the-mud," came to mind.

By combining a pollywog kick and a certain amount of arm flailing, he managed to wriggle out of his parachute harness and thence to firmer ground. *Best divest myself of this outer layer,* he said to himself.

MacSweeny then took off his heavy winter flying boots, jacket, and helmet. He located some fairly clean water, and with his bargain-basement scarf, did his best to clean up his face and his now not-so-sparkling blue eyes. His cadet uniform, worn underneath, was only slightly damp and hardly soiled at all, considering what he had just experienced.

He stuffed his muddy flying clothes under a bush, carefully noting the location, shook out the parachute, and folded it as compactly as he could. It was still a mess but at least a smaller one.

He started walking down the dirt road that paralleled the power lines, carrying the muddy parachute. In less than a mile he encountered an elderly farmer on a tractor.

"Could you give me a lift to the Naval Air Station?" MacSweeny asked. "I've had a little trouble." (This was like the duty officer at Pearl Harbor calling up Admiral Kimmel: "Sir, we've had a bit of trouble over here at the harbor.")

The farmer hesitated a moment and then replied, "Reckon

I can help you out, son. Be glad to run you down to the highway where you can catch a bus. That air station's a mite too far. Besides, this tractor ain't allowed on paved roads. Jus' climb up on the fender."

MacSweeny did not bother with any explanations, and the old man apparently needed none. Maybe he figured that, if someone wanted to carry around a muddy mess of cotton and rope, it was their own business. MacSweeny likewise failed to see any advantage in blurting out, "Hey, look at me! I just fell out of an airplane." It didn't seem to be an appropriate conversation opener. It would be hard enough to explain all this to his instructor and fellow cadets when he got back aboard the base.

During the short tractor ride to the highway, MacSweeny thought back to his recent earth landing. He did not recall any particular shock from the parachute opening. *It must have opened just as I hit that snowbank,* he decided. It was a difficult mystery to solve since no eyes had actually witnessed his disappearing act. However, later investigation concluded that he had indeed hit at almost the exact instant that his chute had opened, judging from the depth MacSweeny had plunged into the snow and mud. Most assuredly, the weekend's snow deposits, along with the subsequent melting, had combined to save his life.

The city bus that picked him up after getting off the tractor was empty save for the driver. Once again, no questions were asked, and no comments from Paratrooper MacSweeny were offered.

A military police pickup truck took MacSweeny from the main gate, where he had gotten off the bus, to the squadron flight line. A brief discussion with the gate sentry as to why the cadet had no liberty card and, therefore, could not come aboard the air station was settled by the sergeant of the guard.

He would drive him to the flight line, liberty card or not. The sergeant's curious stares were met with quiet indifference.

The sergeant had to have recognized the mess MacSweeny was carrying as a parachute, but no one had ever walked up to the main gate before with one tucked under his arm. It would have been beneath him to ask the obvious question, particularly of a cadet. He would surely have heard that old line that went, "My chute didn't work, so I'm bringing it back to get another one."

In any event, with whatever great difficulty and restraint, the sergeant kept his silence and deposited the cadet and his untidy bundle at the paraloft.

MacSweeny's first action, quite naturally for him, was to turn in his parachute, since they had to be checked out and in before and after each flight.

"Jesus Christ! What the hell did you do to it?" The sailor in charge of the paraloft was furious. "You'll get some demerits for this."

Since some cadet accidentally spilled his chute almost daily, it was obvious to the sailor that this cadet had done just that, only he had spilled it into mud. With a glare that suggested that MacSweeny was the type that went to the bathroom too near the house, the sailor grudgingly accepted the untidy mess and crossed off MacSweeny's name.

The next stop was the men's room, where a more complete grooming was accomplished. Sparkling anew, MacSweeny then presented himself to the desk in Operations, behind which sat the very important chief flight instructor, who was busily talking on the telephone in an intense manner.

"Pardon me, Sir, Cadet Mac—"

"Not now, son. I'm right in the middle of something."

He continued talking on the phone, indicating to MacSweeny that their conversation was over. Chief Flight was an extremely important person, both king and the court of last appeals, all in one. MacSweeny's attire and demeanor in no way resembled that of anyone who had just fallen four thousand feet into a snowbank, ridden a tractor, caught a bus, and hopped a ride in an MP's pickup truck. Consequently, the chief went back to the business at hand, which was to locate a cadet, missing and presumed dead.

MacSweeny, on the other hand, had no way of knowing that his instructor had not seen him on the ground, waving to confirm that he was alive and well. He did realize that they did not know he was back safely and that he should check in with someone. MacSweeny decided to look for his instructor. A quick check of the schedules board showed that Lieutenant MacCarthy had returned from his nine o'clock flight and then taken off again. MacSweeny headed for the cadet ready room to further ponder the situation.

A very grim-faced Lieutenant MacCarthy had indeed taken off again, this time with two other Stearmans to aid in his search for the fallen cadet. He had also instituted a vehicular ground search, which had already left the air station. Both groups could only hope for the best.

MacSweeny entered the cadet ready room without fanfare. He was unnoticed by the two dozen or so future navy pilots sitting around the room. He sauntered over to a hot bridge game in progress, where four of the inner 14B group were seated. The card players were Al Fox, Harry Owens, Bud Rich (later of Blue Angels fame), and I, Don Tooker.

"Hi, Iwo, how did your A-1 go?" Rich inquired.

MacSweeny hesitated for a moment, his mind grasping for the right answer. All he could come up with was, "I'm not sure you're going to believe this."

He was not quite ready to explain all that had just happened to him. He did not know whether he was in trouble or not, or exactly what to do. "I'm waiting to talk to my instructor."

The bridge game continued for a few moments, and then Rich spoke again. "Hey, Iwo, how about taking my hand? I've got to get dressed for my hop."

Bridge did not seem quite appropriate at the time, but then, what would? MacSweeny sat down and picked up Rich's cards. Several hands later, he glanced up to see his instructor walk past the ready room door. He was very thin-lipped and, oddly, still wearing his parachute. MacSweeny waved and made his way toward the door. A bewildered Lieutenant MacCarthy met him halfway across the room.

"MacSweeny! You're all right! How'd you get here? Your chute . . . ?"

Confusion reigned supreme. MacCarthy's emotions ran the gamut from extreme joy to anger, then from frustration to curiosity, before finally settling on relief. He had never been more thankful to see anyone in his life. His fourteen months of combat in the South Pacific were a lark compared to the events of this day.

MacSweeny hurriedly told the entire story, even mentioning his series of rides back to the air station, the return of his chute, and the location of his stashed winter flying gear.

"When did you open your chute? I never saw it at all."

"I was pretty low, I think, maybe a hundred feet, I'm not sure. I must have hit the snowbank about the same time it opened." Finally beginning to appreciate the lieutenant's distress, MacSweeny added, magnanimously, " I guess a white chute would be hard to see against the snow."

Chief Flight was informed at once and the air and ground searches recalled. Lieutenant MacCarthy soon repaired to the officers' club bar, even though it was only eleven o'clock in the morning. Chief Flight then called MacSweeny into his office.

"Son, you must know that you're a very lucky cadet. I've spoken with Lieutenant MacCarthy, and he feels that from now on, perhaps you'd be more comfortable flying with a different instructor. I'll make the necessary arrangements."

FOR MACSWEENY, the story was out. He was right about the other cadets not believing him at first. But big news like that traveled fast at the air station. He had to recite the entire episode from beginning to end many times, often to the same audience.

In reenacting the drama, it was determined that the cuff of MacSweeny's right glove had accidentally caught and released the safety-belt toggle as he changed hands from the left side of the cockpit to the right side, in his effort to get a better grip.

But one vital question remained: Would MacSweeny lose some of his newly found prestige by having fallen out of his airplane? Not even a little bit. In fact, he became the coolest one ever, for now "Iwo Jima" MacSweeny, credited with action in the Pacific, had made a successful parachute jump on his very first flight!

10 Engine Failure, His and Hers

"MAYDAY! MAYDAY! MAYDAY! This is Bonanza November Eight Nine Charlie in the mountains east of Julian VOR, seventy-five hundred feet. Total engine failure! Anyone this frequency come in!"

Almost immediately: "Roger, Eight Nine Charlie, this is Navy Miramar Tower. If you are transponder equipped, squawk emergency."

Below, the rugged terrain made any walk-away-from-landing an impossibility. I glanced at my copilot, who also happened to be my wife. She was terrified and had every right to be.

"Look for anything flat like a road or a field, Peri," I ordered, just to give her something else to think about.

The look of terror in her eyes told me I was on my own. It was her *first* engine failure and my fourth, but that really didn't make it any easier for either of us. The sheer canyon walls dotted with giant boulders dictated an immediate 180-degree course reversal. The black clouds overhead completely screened out the sun, making the sky very dark although it was only mid-morning. Rain on the windscreen reduced the forward visibility to about three miles. The altimeter needle was moving slowly counter-clockwise past seven thousand feet.

"November Eight Nine Charlie, roger your Mayday. Say your position again. This is Miramar Tower. Are you squawking emer . . . ."

Their response was weak and garbled as the transmission faded completely. We were already too low behind the mountains just west of San Diego for the line-of-sight VHF communication. Giving up on the radio, I concentrated on the best plan of action. I figured the ground elevation must be around three thousand feet, leaving us with only about four thousand feet to negotiate before our coming rendezvous with the rocks below.

We had departed the Aeroclub at the Marine Corps Air Station, El Toro, California, some thirty minutes earlier, in our 1955 single-engine, V-tailed Bonanza. Our destination was Loreto, in Baja California, for a combined business and pleasure trip. It was the day after Christmas, 1984.

Peri was having a really rough time, lips pressed tightly together, her face drained of color; I could tell she was sure she was going to die. Exiting the box canyon in our soundless glide, we entered another less rugged but very narrow valley. I spotted a tiny, winding road; no good, not enough straightaway. Farther on, some rugged fields of brush, probably hiding ditches and more boulders.

As the altimeter needle passed five thousand feet, I tried to give my wife a reassuring smile. She was unconvinced, staring transfixed, straight ahead. I could easily guess what she was thinking: *How much does it hurt when you crash?*

About two thousand feet of usable altitude left, maybe two to three minutes, I guessed. Not enough time to check

The author refuels Beechcraft Bonanza November 89 Charlie on the morning of the fateful flight.

the map for the exact height of the terrain. My thirty-five years of flying experience would have to get us through. On our outbound heading we had passed some dirt roads and several small airstrips. But how far back?

I wondered momentarily what had gone wrong. The engine failure had been sudden and complete and, in my mind, catastrophic. There had been no way to restart it and no time to do anything but switch fuel tanks, and that had not helped. I remembered the previous "gripe sheet," which mentioned a somewhat lower than average oil pressure, about 70 PSI, well within the normal range of 60 to 90 PSI—so that wasn't the problem. Paul, the chief pilot of the Aeroclub, had reminded me that N89C had not flown in several weeks while awaiting some part not related to the engine.

I had neither the time nor the inclination to go back over all of my previous engine failures, but the experience gained from them would prove invaluable. The first one, in a Piper

Cub when I was twenty years old, occurred just after takeoff, the worst possible time. I got away with a cardinal sin: turning back toward the departed runway. (When you own your airplane, you sometimes do dumb things like that.) Fortunately, there was a short auxiliary runway requiring only about 120 degrees of course reversal. I had sailed over the sagebrush at the Cable Claremont Airport with about fifteen feet of clearance, leveling the wings at the last possible second and touching down on the very end. My frightened passenger (an old high school girlfriend) and I picked up the tail and dragged the Cub back to the parking area. The disgusted look from Dewey Cable, the airport manager, said it all. Still, I did learn from that experience, as we shall see.

Up ahead to the right, perpendicular to our heading, a straight line appeared. A road? No, by God, a small grass strip.

"That's got to be the glider strip at Warner Springs, Peri."

Her eyes were asking me, "Will we make it?"

"We'll try to set her down there. Tighten your safety belt, Babe . . . real tight!"

For a nonaviator, my wife had a fair amount of flying experience. She had flown with me a lot and could hold a course and maintain an altitude pretty well. However, until this flight, she had had no experience with emergencies or training in emergency procedures. To remedy this situation, she had recently enrolled in a "Pinch Hitter's Course for Wives of Pilots" at the Aeroclub at El Toro. The idea was that, if I suddenly keeled over while on a flight, she would have enough training and ability to take over the controls, switch to the proper radio channel, squawk emergency on the IFF, and land the aircraft, hopefully in one piece.

That was all to the good, but not much help if I keeled over now. She had trained in a Cessna 152, and we were flying in a much higher performance Beechcraft Bonanza. The latter was almost twice as fast and hard to slow down to a safe approach speed, and it had retractable landing gear. However, my copilot had done well in pilot school. She had about fifteen hours' total flight time, knew how to work the radios, knew which side of the aircraft to enter (the one with the door), and had soloed. Peri had made three landings without her instructor aboard. The bad news was that he had only *discussed,* not demonstrated, emergency approaches and landings. This would be her first such experience.

With a little over fifteen hundred feet left, I figured I would make a left-hand approach and land to the west, which should be into the wind. With the rain, there was no way to know wind direction for certain. But playing the altitude by S-turning is taught in most every primary flight-training syllabus. *Luck is with us after all,* I thought to myself.

As I began a gentle left-hand turn into the strip, I looked down on an alarming development. Someone was pushing a glider onto the grass strip about one-third of the way down from our intended touchdown spot. The lucky feeling was, it seemed, sadly premature.

"Damn, Peri, we'll have to go around. That glider's got the strip blocked from this direction."

For a moment I had forgotten that we, too, were a glider, an inefficient one at that, and a go-around would require engine power. There was only one chance, a slim one. I executed a hard and immediate reversal turn, careful to keep the nose down and not lose flying speed, to avoid the fatal spin that can occur in these circumstances. Now we were too low, with no altitude to S-turn, no margin for error. We headed for the other end of the strip for a landing to the east, which would give us two-thirds of usable runway.

The steep bank as we turned on a very low final would

An alarming development: the glider on the small grass strip at Warner Springs.

have scared any pilot who was paying attention, as I certainly was. The ground was rushing up, the right wing tip scraping the tops of the sagebrush.

"Oh, Don!" screamed Peri.

That said it all. This was the moment of truth. I rolled the wings level, slapped the landing gear lever down, and prayed that there would be enough time for the gear to fully extend. We touched down on the absolute end of the strip, just past a drainage ditch. The sound of the wheels rolling on the ground was a huge relief. We were hot, what with a no-flap landing, as I prepared to intentionally ground-loop into the brush on the right to avoid hitting the glider.

However, at that exact moment, the glider suddenly moved forward and off the runway. We sailed silently by two very startled glider pilots, our propeller frozen in the vertical position. I braked to a stop at the far end of the runway and turned off the mags by habit.

We sat there in silence—stunned—and then we unstrapped and embraced emotionally. Peri was sobbing quietly and, like me, grateful to be alive. On shaky legs, we walked over to thank the two pilots for moving their glider in the nick of time, only to learn that they had neither seen nor heard us. It had been just lucky timing. They were merely practicing glider positioning onto the runway and into takeoff position, in expectations of a sunnier tomorrow.

Postflight inspection revealed a completely sheared crankshaft. My instincts had been right. The engine could not have been restarted.

I telephoned the FAA and Miramar Naval Air station and told them we were safely on the ground at Warner Springs. They thanked me for the information.

The Aeroclub was not nearly as appreciative. They had to launch a two-engine bird big enough to carry their mechanic and pilot, along with Peri and me. When they had arrived and tried to move the propeller, they discovered that the engine was scrambled. The propeller was immovable and stuck in the twelve o'clock position. They were impressed no small amount when they reviewed our approach, go-around, and touchdown rollout. A few feet less runway, and that drainage ditch would have mangled both the Bonanza and us.

On our flight back to the El Toro air station in another Aeroclub aircraft, I felt pretty good and proud of having saved the airplane, not to mention our lives. I had exercised good judgment and a fair amount of flying skill, learned from almost seven thousand flying hours.

Then it hit me, that sometimes indefinable element we all talk about, *luck*. If the crankshaft had let go just a few seconds later, the quick reversal turn would not have gotten us back out of that canyon. We would have had to take on those mountain walls and boulders, and most assuredly would have lost the whole ballgame.

EPILOGUE

The engine of the Beechcraft Bonanza was eventually replaced and the aircraft flown to the airport at Corona, California. We kept on flying N89C for another year until its owner moved it to Northern California. Peri and I still fly together, despite her sometimes white knuckles. But she will always fly with me, she says, "because you're a good pilot," and, Lord knows, a lucky one, too. Besides, now she has had *her* first emergency landing.

11 | Race One, You're on Fire

THE LOCATION IS Phoenix, Arizona, and the date is 19 March 1994. The event is the first Phoenix 500, the air races for unlimited propeller-driven aircraft. Air racing is the fastest motor sport in the world. For aviation fans, these competitors provide the ultimate in thrills as they risk their lives to be the fastest over the race course.

Six World War II fighters are flying around eight ground-marker pylons arranged in an oval pattern at speeds up to 430 miles an hour and as low as fifty feet above the ground. The contenders are three P-51 Mustangs, two British-built Sea Furies, and one Super Corsair.

This is the second of the day's three heat races. Two of the six laps have been completed. Long-time Reno Air Races participant Howard Pardue is in the lead in one of the Sea Furies, with the Super Corsair running second and closing rapidly.

At the controls of the famous gull-winged Corsair is Kevin Eldridge, who at thirty-two is the youngest active pilot competing in the unlimited category of air racing. He has already flown most of the World War II warbirds, many of which have been restored by Fighter Rebuilders of Chino, California. This is his seventh air race, and he is confident of overtaking the Sea Fury and thus earning a start in the final heat of the next day, with a chance of winning the Gold Trophy.

THE RACE had started smoothly with some able assistance from the airborne race coordinator, Bob Hoover. Pardue's Sea Fury had gotten a great start and had jumped out to an early lead. Kevin and his Race One ground crew's strategy was very basic: "Find out who's the fastest and go after him." It works for the best drivers every year at the Indianapolis 500 auto races, and the Race One team figured it would work for them.

Laps one and two were routine, if flying so fast and close to the ground can be called that. In fact, from some vantage points it appeared that the fighters were actually flying below the terrain level.

"Race One, from ground crew. How are your temperatures?" A second's pause, and the response: "A-ah . . . roger, they're running about normal." They would all remember his slight hesitation, later.

Entering the third lap with his eyes glued to the fighter just a few feet ahead, Kevin felt a slight shudder. *Slipstream or a burble from the high G forces,* he reasoned.

The next vibration was much more severe and felt like a car plunging over a high curb. Violent shaking was followed by a sudden loss of power. Instinctively, Kevin pulled back on the stick and closed the throttle, effectively trading airspeed for some altitude and a little time to sort things out. The 400-plus-mph trade brought him up to almost five thousand feet.

"Mayday! Mayday! From Race One. Looks like I've got an engine failure."

"Roger your Mayday, Race One," responded both the

ground crew and Hoover, the airborne race coordinator. Their acknowledgment brought slight comfort; in reality, their only functions were to watch and wait and in some way possibly help the stricken pilot. The Mayday from Race One served to inform the other five pilots still racing, along with the race coordinator, that he was in distress, leaving the race, and would most likely be attempting an emergency landing very shortly.

In the cockpit, Kevin's eyes swept across the instrument panel. No surprises there. He was already acutely aware that his engine had failed. The violent vibrations had diminished, but, at idle, the huge engine could not deliver enough power to sustain flight. Grey smoke was starting to fill the cockpit, and some trailing smoke was confirmed by the ground crew. As he leveled off, Kevin began to mentally set up for a dead-stick landing on the nearby airstrip, figuring that a burned piston might be the culprit—not at all uncommon in the high-compression engines used in air racing.

"Race One, we're seeing some flame underneath the fuse-lage," this radioed from his ground crew.

"Roger, understand, from Race One."

The belly was the one place Kevin could not see from the cockpit. Suddenly, his headset was filled with the words that every fighter pilot dreads, particularly those sitting directly behind 150 gallons of high-test gasoline and ether.

"Race One, you're on fire! Bail out! Bail out!"

Kevin could now feel the heat coming from the engine section as more smoke streamed into the cockpit. No more time for radio transmissions. He quickly disconnected his oxygen hose and radio cords, released his safety belt and shoulder straps, and banked the Corsair away from the crowded grandstands. Then he trimmed the fighter to keep it in a reasonably level attitude and cranked open the canopy.

There are no ejection seats in World War II fighters. He would have to climb up and out of the cockpit and attempt to dive or bail out over the side. Any such maneuver would likely slam him right into the tail structure, as it had many a luckless pilot in World War II, but his options were nil.

As he tried to stand up and push himself out of the cockpit, the 250-mph slipstream literally blew him out of the seat and slammed his body onto the surface of the tail's horizontal stabilizer. The impact knocked off his protective helmet and oxygen mask, stunning him momentarily. Regaining his senses, he looked for the parachute ripcord D ring, only to find it missing. It apparently had been knocked loose in his collision with the tail.

Panic set in when he realized that he could not open his chute. But as he groped wildly with both hands for the ripcord, the problem evaporated. Magically, the chute opened as if some unseen hand had pulled the D ring for him. He would figure this out later . . . . (Experts generally agreed that the force of his tumbling through space had provided enough inertia to force the ripcord and D ring to extend and thus open the chute.)

As he hung in his harness, slowly descending toward a sagebrush-covered area, he took a careful inventory of his person and equipment and realized that some very serious problems still faced him. Indeed, his troubles were far from over. Glancing upward, he observed that two panels of his parachute were ripped, promising a hard landing, for sure. The next discoveries were even worse. He could feel the broken bone in his right arm, bent at a sickening angle. Upon pulling up one of the trouser legs on his flight suit, he could see why his left foot was pointed in the wrong direction; two bones protruding grotesquely out of the side of his leg. He would have only one good leg to break his fall upon landing.

Kevin's mind was full of misgivings as he fell. He had no

way of knowing how much faster than normal the torn chute was letting him fall. For that matter, he had never experienced *any* parachute jump, normal or otherwise; this was his first. He didn't know what to expect. Something else that Kevin did not know was that his neck was broken.

As the ground rushed up to meet him, he raised his injured leg and tried to land on the good right one. He hit heavily in some fairly soft dirt and rolled over immediately, effectively collapsing the chute. When he tried to get up, he found that he could not.

In a few minutes the ambulance and the medics arrived. The attendants gently removed his chute and made him as comfortable as possible. Once his neck was stabilized, he was carefully placed on a stretcher and taken by helicopter to a nearby hospital. The medical team reported that the only question he asked of them was, "My plane didn't hit anyone, did it?" Assured that it had not, he relaxed and let the injected painkiller do its work.

ALTHOUGH KEVIN ELDRIDGE's luck that day might be called mixed, he would fully recover from his injuries. His souvenirs of the event include a steel plate in his right arm, scars where the bone pierced his left leg, and memories of three months in a head-and-neck stabilizer anchored by four stainless steel needles in his skull.

His chute opened, he missed the spectators, and he lived to fly again.

A preliminary accident investigation determined that a broken master rod caused one or more cylinders to fail, explaining the engine failure and subsequent fire.

I HAD MET Kevin Eldridge before the events described here. Fighter Rebuilders, Inc. had given me a certificate for a demo ride in a P-51 at its Chino, California, airport facility. Since navy and marine pilots hardly ever get a chance to fly one another's service aircraft, I was keenly interested. Kevin piloted the demo flight.

For a demo flight, the hitchhiker rides piggyback in a small seat located just behind the pilot. It's uncomfortable, noisy as hell, and exhilarating—even though the hitchhiker has no access to the controls.

I mentioned to Kevin, by way of making conversation, that if we met in a dogfight—he in the P-51, me in my Corsair— he might be embarrassed. Of course, he took that "throwing down the gauntlet" remark seriously and replied with a demonstration of low-altitude acrobatics that *fully* displayed the attributes of the North American–built fighter.

On the strength of that experience, among others, I have decided that in my next life I shall be a civilian pilot who tests and checks out vintage aircraft. Some of the planes that I (and Kevin, in *his* next life—although he has already flown all of them in this one) will be flying are:

B-26 Marauder	BF-109 Messerschmitt
P-51	F7F Tigercat
F4F Wildcat	B-17 Flying Fortress
P-38 Lightning	Hawker Sea Fury
Japanese Zero	F4U Corsair
F8F Bearcat	B-25 Mitchell
P-47 Thunderbolt	Spitfire Mark IX

With the ungovernable and imperishable one-upmanship of the career aviator, I will relish the opportunity to reply if anybody innocently asks, "And what are you flying now?"

EPILOGUE

After his spectacular accident, Kevin was grateful to be alive, but, like many young pilots of his breed, he could not wait to

Race pilot Kevin Eldridge—wearing a "halo" neck brace—and the author pose in front of an F4U-4 Corsair in April 1994 at Eldridge's home field in Chino, California.

get back to flying and racing other World War II aircraft. I have stayed in touch with him. He has since married, but that has not slowed him down in the slightest. He's still flying vintage aircraft. He says it's a pretty tough job but someone has to do it.

12 Black Sheep Eight Misses a Party

A CCIDENTS HAVE BEEN associated with air shows, but most of them happen at the air show, not on the way to an air show. This story is about one that happened en route.

Eight Marine Corps pilots in single-seater F4U Corsairs were assigned to participate in the Annual SeaFair celebration sponsored by the city of Seattle, Washington. If you come from the Northwest, this extravaganza needs no introduction. Less fortunate souls should know that the Seattle city fathers, along with the city mothers, pull out all the stops: parades, parties, dinners, speeches, air shows—almost anything festive and exciting. It resembles in some ways a New Orleans Mardi Gras, without the Cajun hot sauce.

Hoping to help with the excitement and most certainly aware of the party part, our group of eight experienced combat veterans departed El Toro, California, in high spirits, enthusiastic about the flight to and from Seattle and certainly the air show itself.

The date was 2 August 1952. The site of the air show was the naval air station at Sand Point, situated on the shores of

Lake Washington, almost in downtown Seattle. However, there were no suitable accommodations for us or our aircraft at Sand Point, so our destination and our home for the three-day excursion was to be the naval air station on Whidbey Island. We planned to refuel at Medford, Oregon, on the way.

Our unit happened to be one of the most famous in the naval service. We were members of Marine fighter squadron VMF-214, the Black Sheep Squadron. Some years later, those who might otherwise never have heard of VMF-214 would be thrilled (I trust) by the many episodes on TV entitled *Baa, Baa, Black Sheep,* starring Robert Conrad.

The flight leader and commanding officer was Maj. M. M. Cook. He was an experienced fighter pilot and well liked by all of the pilots. His nickname was "Sir."

On his wing was Capt. Shelby Forrest, nicknamed "Whiskey." He had an amazing ability to recall many ribald songs and verses, featured in many a morale-building happy hour.

Leading the second section in the No. 3 slot was Capt. "Nobby" Norbom, a reserve officer, veteran of World War II, and All-California fullback in both high school and junior college in Pasadena. His chief claim to fame was that he had dated June Christy when she was a cheerleader in high school and later when she became famous as a singer in the Stan Kenton band.

Capt. "Scotty" Stevenson was also a reserve officer, recalled because of the Korean conflict; he owned a dry-cleaning business in the greater Seattle area. His presence in the flight was considered essential for his knowledge of local sightseeing and activities. (As it turned out, we didn't need it. On our one night of liberty, we were happily ambushed at the American Legion Club, where we had stopped for a drink, and were entertained through the next morning by the hospitable people of Mt.Vernon.)

But back to the flight: Leading the second division of four aircraft was Capt. Don Hinshaw, a pilot of considerable skill, as we shall soon see. A handsome and capable flight leader, Don was a professional career officer who had gained some notoriety during his previous Korean overseas tour for firing on a couple of aircraft that dove on his two-Corsair section from above—only to discover later that his "one destroyed, one probable" had been British Sea Furies from the carrier HMS *Glorious*. The Brits were able to land aboard safely. Don duly wrote an apology, but nobody ever explained why the British pilots had made a run on the Americans in the first place. Fighter pilots from both nations had a lot of fun relating the story in their respective messes.

On Hinshaw's wing was another captain, "Long John" Elledge. Since he stood six-foot-six, the nickname was inevitable. As a career officer, John was a quiet, studious, and intelligent pilot. He drove a brand-new Mercury sedan, the color of tomato puree, which did not harm his bachelor standing.

Flying a modest but flawless wing position and leading the second section was another captain whose flymanship knew no bounds. He had recently accepted a regular commission and was, by his own admission, an excellent aviator. He was, of course, me.

Flying in the Number Eight position was 1st Lt. Jim Laseter. He was an exceptional pilot and also had just been accepted into the regular Marine Corps establishment. He had green eyes, was ruggedly built, and possessed a world-class natural grin. He had been a first stringer on the naval air base football team at Pensacola, Florida, while a cadet. He was also my next-door neighbor in Laguna Beach, a distinction that has no bearing whatsoever on his featured role in this story.

Blessed with all of the qualities aforementioned, the eight pilots joined up in a comfortable formation, once airborne from El Toro, and proceeded up the California coast to their first stop, Medford, Oregon, to refuel. The weather was briefed to be clear, and spirits were high. The sight of eight World War II bent-wing fighters evenly spaced in formation is truly a beautiful and memorable thing to behold, whether one is a pilot or a normal person. Being part of such an uplifting spectacle was pure joy. All radios, engines, and other necessary equipment were functioning perfectly.

Promptly and exactly at the California-Oregon border, the weather returned to "smotts," in the words of "Whiskey" Forrest.

"How does it know? He had radioed the skipper, Major Cook.

"Don't exactly know, Black Sheep Two," Cook had replied. "Maybe California has a better chamber of commerce."

Because of the deteriorating weather, some deviations from the general flight plan were in order. Ceiling height is critical when flying on a VFR (Visual Flight Rules) flight plan. It must be at least a thousand feet above the terrain or sea level. Even though the aerologist at El Toro had promised good weather in his forecast, the ceiling had lowered to around a thousand feet. The word *around* is significant, and in such events only one opinion counts anyway: that of the flight leader, whose credibility here gained somewhat from his also being the CO.

The flight swung out over the ocean and let down beneath the offending clouds. Somewhere in the vicinity of Crescent City the flight spotted a small break in the cloud cover and scooted into and through a canyon flying eastward. This route led to Grants Pass and then to the Rogue River. A little farther on we spotted the welcome runway at Medford, Oregon. So far, so good.

Our flight leader, ever confident, decided to demonstrate a carrier-type break. Directly over the runway at three hundred feet in a right echelon of eight, we broke at twenty-second intervals, landing smartly in perfect alignment. There wasn't much of a crowd observing us, but that didn't matter. We knew we had done it up right.

The precision landing demonstration completed, two airport ground personnel directed us into the parking area. They appeared to us to need a little more stimulus, so on "Sir"'s command, we all folded our wings simultaneously, as only navy carrier aircraft can do. No one on the ground seemed misty-eyed with admiration. Perhaps they had eight Corsairs dropping in on their small civilian field every day.

My job in the squadron was that of material officer, a job that ranked (still does) right up there with the common cold and comes with the title of "responsible officer," which could have career-ending consequences. I was signed out for all squadron equipment except the airplanes themselves. It also fell to me, during cross-country flights such as this, to carry the U.S. Government gas chits with which to purchase our gasoline and oil from the supplier—in this case, Medford Airport.

Our squadron had sent a dispatch ahead to the Medford airport and received confirmation that 100-octane fuel and oil were available in the quantity requested. I searched out the airport manager, a former army pilot, and was horrified to learn that all of the 100-octane gas had been contaminated by a recent rainstorm. I could accept this lamebrain excuse but not the fact that he had failed to inform us of the situa-

Eight Marine Corsairs of the famous Black Sheep Squadron await refueling at Medford, Oregon, on their way to the annual Seattle Airshow in 1952.

tion. Our thirsty fighters were quite low on petrol, so we would need an alternate plan. We had enough gas for about ninety minutes of flying time at low power settings.

I relayed this disturbing information to the skipper and thought for a few minutes that he was going to kill the messenger, as it were. But he calmed down and we focused on the solution rather than the problem. We both realized that getting eight Corsairs stuck in Oregon en route to an air show in the State of Washington was not a career-enhancing option. While the other pilots were catching up on soft drinks and sandwiches and utilizing the rest-stop facilities, the major and his material officer powwowed. What *were* the options?

We could not make it all the way to Seattle (NAS Whidbey Island) or even Portland with any reserve fuel. Our now suspect airport manager said he thought Salem, to the north, had 100-octane. All airports normally have plenty of 80-octane fuel, but our Corsairs, powered with Pratt & Whitney R-2800 engines with 2,250 horsepower, could not use the lower-rated fuel. The engines were actually doing us a favor by agreeing to run on 100-octane gas; we just couldn't use full power on takeoff or, for that matter, ever. The engines actually were specified to use 115/145 high-octane fuel.

We reached the airport manager at the Salem Municipal Airport by phone. After checking his fuel availability, he allowed as how he could sell us a maximum of 150 gallons per aircraft, twelve hundred gallons, but that it would wipe out his supply of 100-octane. He mentioned something about "anything for the boys in the service" and to come on up. I assumed from that that he was not an ex-army pilot.

The weather report from CAA (now FAA) foretold of some nasty weather between Medford and Salem. We would have to climb up through the overcast, fly above the clouds, and then let down through the same overcast to make an approach at our refueling destination. The fuel margin, or reserve, would just barely be legal by federal regulations. We would be flying by instrument flight rules under positive radar control once we reached an altitude where we could be painted (that is, seen) by the radar controllers. We were reminded rather dramatically that both Medford and, to some extent, Salem were in a valley bordered by the Pacific Coast Range on the west and the Cascade Range to the east. These mountain ranges rose from five to nine thousand feet. Thus, any deviation from the exact course upon entering the Willamette Valley could be disastrous. We had to rely on our Medford departure radar controllers to pick us up at around five to six thousand feet, since their radar, like our VHF radios, operated on the line-of-sight principle. They would keep us on course and start us down for the letdown into the Salem Airport.

However, assuming that we negotiated the Willamette Valley without hitting a mountain on either side, we still had nervous twitches at the thought of the final approach, in the soup, to Salem. One reason for this reflex was that at Salem no precision approach was available. All it had was the relatively primitive low-frequency radio range.

This navigational aid was in use in the late 1920s and perfected mostly by airmail pilots along with Jimmy Doolittle in the 1930s. A four-legged pattern with two intersecting beams was transmitted from a ground station. The two beams intersected close to the landing airport, enabling a pilot to pick up a beam and ride it into the field. If he deviated to the left, for example, he would receive the aural letter "A" in his headset; to the right, he'd hear an "N." Thus the expression, "You're on the beam," originated with this navigational equipment.

All we had to do was to get eight Corsairs on the beam.

We filed our flight plan, manned aircraft, taxied out, and took off in single file, making a circling rendezvous. We departed picturesque Medford Airport to the north. To my knowledge, there had been no fond or tearful farewells. My only regret was that I had not had time to inspect the airport's excellent restroom facilities, the duties of responsible officer having taken precedence. We were looking at a fifty-minute flight for the 160-mile leg, with the climb-out and letdown time figured in.

Everyone today is familiar with the navy's Blue Angels flight demonstration team, particularly their precision and skill while flying their patented close-wing positions. They would have been envious of the Black Sheep's parade formation on the climb-out from Medford in heavy clouds, with each pilot knowing what could happen if his aircraft got separated. Every pilot had his wing overlapping that of another, with his wingtip only about three feet from the pilot's cockpit ahead. With serious mountains on both sides, only one thing mattered: Don't lose sight of the guy in front of you! The leader alone had no tight-wing-formation duties. He was free as a bird. All he had to do was lead seven other aircraft exactly on the proper course and not think about the other pilots whose lives depended on his skill.

The radar controller's calm voice came through our helmets: "Marine Black Sheep Flight, we have you on radar, thirty-five miles north of Medford at fifty-five hundred feet. Confirm squawking Code 45 (IFF) and continue your climb. Tops are reported at seventy-five hundred feet. Report VFR on-top."

"Roger, Medford Departure Control. Will report on top." Everyone, from what I could ascertain, seemed at ease and no one except the skipper had come on the radio. I wondered if there was any puckering going on in the other cockpits.

"Medford Control, this is Black Sheep Flight. We're on top at seventy-eight hundred feet." No response was necessary from Departure Control.

The sun was a welcome, dazzling, brilliant ball of fire. The flight immediately spread out to a much more relaxed wing formation. It was time to check everything and to tell ourselves, "Hey now, that wasn't so tough, was it?" Then a sobering thought entered our minds: "We've got to do this whole damn thing again, going *down* the hill." No rest for the wicked.

After about twenty minutes of scenic mountain viewing, the flight leader came up on the air, having been told by Medford Departure that we should begin our letdown momentarily and descend into the Salem airport.

"This is Black Sheep One. Is anyone receiving the Salem radio range? I'm just getting static."

No one answered for several seconds as each pilot adjusted

his "coffee grinder" handle to the only navigational aid in the cockpit. My signal was weak but clear; still, I hesitated to answer. If I had the only workable radio, I would have to lead seven other guys down through the weather, passing precisely between the mountain ranges. Even for the responsible officer, this was a serious challenge. Before I had to reach a decision, Captain Hinshaw, of Anglo-American relations fame, saved the day.

"I've got the Salem range fairly loud and clear."

"OK, Don, bring your division on up and my four will join on you." For a tense moment I thought he was talking to the other Don, me.

"Roger, Skipper, I've got the lead. Flight, let's stay in nice and tight on this letdown." Talk about unnecessary advice. It was like suggesting that smoother landings are made with wheels down and locked.

"Black Sheep Flight, this is Medford Departure Control. You are over your letdown point. You are cleared to the Salem Airport, cleared to descend from your present altitude and for a low-frequency radio range approach. Be advised that runway 34 is in use. Contact the tower on 122.9. We've advised Salem that you're inbound with eight aircraft and they are holding all local traffic. Good luck!" It was nice to know that the radar control folks knew how tough this landing was going to be.

Hinshaw rogered his acknowledgment and, easing power very gradually, we started down the long hill. As we entered the other world, the bright sun disappeared, along with each fighter pilot's nonchalance.

"This is Black Sheep Leader. Let's stay off the radio so I can hear the signal better. I have us right on the beam center now . . . stay in tight." At this point each pilot would have folded his wings if Don had deemed it appropriate. I lined up the two pilots' heads in front of me and tried to make gentle power and control corrections, to make it easier work for the pilots following me.

The letdown by my emotional watch took about two hours, but by the cockpit clock, only sixteen minutes. We broke out from the clouds over a lush green valley at about fourteen hundred feet above the ground. Our parade formation was still flawless as we passed over the landing runway and broke smartly from a right echelon for our landings.

Once safely on the ground, I chatted briefly with a civilian transient pilot flying a twin Beechcraft. He said he had never seen such a beautiful precise formation. I told him we always flew like that.

Don had done a superb job—one that each of us should be expected to do, although usually there was a larger margin of error. One by one the other pilots shuffled by to tell him so. I thanked him later, as my trip to the men's room was long overdue. Only after the rest stop did I verify that suitable av-gas *was* available. It looked as though we were all going to make it to that party in Seattle.

A sandwich and a hot cup of coffee really hit the spot as I thought over the just-completed hop. Some forty-seven years later, that short Medford-to-Salem flight always brings me some satisfaction, along with an appreciation of Don's flying abilities. I never dwell on what might have happened if that radio beam had bent, as they were wont to do, or if the range had ceased to transmit for a few minutes. No room for error, and no errors.

We enjoyed the small-town atmosphere of the Salem airport. Everyone was cordial and wanted to know why we were in Salem and where we were headed. The onlookers, pilots mostly, were more than familiar with our bent-wing birds and wondered if they were hard to fly. Of course, to us they were not; it was a piece of cake. Whenever anyone inquired, our replies were consonant with the official Marine Corps line: "Yes, it is both challenging and rewarding to fly this dependable Chance-Vought-built aircraft."

The refueling took over an hour, allowing some serious relaxing by the other seven pilots. For the responsible officer, it was business as usual. After a short hassle with the airport manager, who had never seen nor heard of U.S. Government gas chits, the matter was settled by calling our Mr. Reliable at the Medford airport. He assured the Salem man that it was quite acceptable tender. Until this point, the Salem manager apparently assumed that almost anyone in the flight would gladly put out the $1,300 that it took to refuel our aircraft. Our pooled resources could not have amounted to much over $350, which in 1952 was about a month's pay for most of us in the military service. I had thirty-eight dollars pinned securely to my underwear.

Now that we had fuel, we knew that the hard part of our cross-country mission was over. The weather forecast for western Washington was CAVU (Ceiling and Visibility Unlimited), every pilot's favorite aerology report. We had already alerted the naval air station at Whidbey Island of our estimated arrival time. A phone call had corrected our ETA, which had been delayed by the unplanned Medford-to-Salem leg. We also confirmed the safe arrival of our support group, the mechanics, spare parts, and tools. Everything was shaping up to our best expectations.

After a short but spirited briefing by the skipper, it was, as in the movies, "Pilots, man your aircraft." Again, we were forced to make single-plane takeoffs because of the very narrow runways. Two-plane section takeoffs are always more fun and more exciting, especially when away from the home field. For sure, they were more "airshowish." We had briefed to make a running rendezvous, departing on a north course toward Seattle and then turning west to the San Juan Islands, where NAS Whidbey was located. The duration of the flight was to be no more than forty-five to fifty minutes.

The Black Sheep Squadron of Pappy Boyington fame taxied out to the main runway, holding short while the pilots ran up their respective engines for the compulsory magneto check. All pilots indicated with their thumbs-up that each was ready for takeoff and departure. For sure, no one wanted to be late to the welcome-aboard party rumored to be awaiting us. For fighter pilots in their twenties, it's a "right stuff" kind of rumor.

I roared down the runway in my usual flawless manner, raised the gear, and closed the canopy. I remember thinking, *Boy, this is what it's all about,* before my aura of pleasure was suddenly shattered.

"Mayday, Mayday. This is Black Sheep Eight. I've got an engine failure."

No one spoke for a moment as we all listened for further information. The news would not be good.

"I'm going in . . . no power at all." Then silence.

I banked sharply to the right, looking for my wingman, Jim, who had taken off just behind me. Our takeoff path took us directly over the town of Salem and I thought, *Oh, God, I hope he's got enough altitude to clear the city.*

A cloud of dust about a mile northeast of the field answered my question. I lowered my wheels and landing flaps so as to fly very slowly over the crash site. After several minutes, the dust cleared and I could see a Corsair sitting forlornly in a plowed field.

"This is Black Sheep Leader. Does anyone have Eight in sight?" The flight leader was already too far north for any visual sighting.

"Affirmative, this is Black Sheep Seven. I'm orbiting the crash. The aircraft is intact. He's bellied in and is evacuating the cockpit. There is no fire yet. He appears to be OK but I can't tell for sure. He just barely missed a farmhouse and . . . ."

"Roger, Seven, from One. Is there a fire crash truck en route? That thing could burn. Black Sheep Flight, we'll orbit the city at five thousand feet. Seven, keep me informed."

"Affirm, Leader, from Seven. He's just standing by the aircraft. I'll make another low pass and check things out. I see a tanker-type fire truck coming. There's still no fire."

I slowed the Corsair as much as I dared and flew by at about a hundred feet (maybe lower) above the crash site. Suddenly, I knew that Jim was all right.

"Black Sheep One. Jim's OK. He just flipped me the bird."

No response, but I could mentally feel the sighs of relief from the Black Sheep Flight. We waited for further instructions from the flight leader.

"Black Sheep Two, from One. Maybe you better go back and land at the airport. I don't know what you can do but some coordination is necessary."

"A-ah, Skipper, I don't think I could do much. Looks like they've got everything under control." The whole flight knew that Whiskey, their star raconteur and party animal, was thinking of the entertainment scheduled for that evening at Whidbey. They also knew orders are orders, particularly when issued by the commanding officer.

It was Lieutenant Laseter, on the ground, who solved the dilemma. He had crawled back into the cockpit to make sure all switches were off. Once in the seat, he had decided that it was safe to switch on the master battery switch along with the VHF radio, coolly ignoring the possibility of the wrecked Corsair erupting into flames.

"This is Black Sheep Eight. I'm fine, Skipper; not a scratch. I don't need any help. There's a fire truck of some kind standing by. Looks like everything is as Whiskey said, under control."

It was clear now that our previously impeccable radio discipline had gone to smotts (like the weather earlier). Jim Laseter continued: "We'll need a crane and a flatbed. I can see to that. The bird's not damaged very much. Can you send an aircraft? I'll join you tomorrow at Whidbey."

The skipper thought this over for a short minute. If he left another aircraft in Salem, he would have only six aircraft available for the air show; plus—and this was the key point— if Whiskey stayed behind, he really should assign *another* aircraft to fly with him. It was standard operating procedure to fly two aircraft together for safety reasons, should one lose a radio or, worse, have to bail out.

"OK, Whiskey, you win. We'll proceed as a flight of seven."

The major had seen through the thin veneer of his wingman's fervent plea, but his decision was based on not leaving two aircraft behind. Besides, it would be hard to put on an air show with only five aircraft.

"Black Sheep Seven, can you join up now? We're orbiting at five thousand feet directly north of the city."

"Affirmative, One. Break, break. You OK, Jim? If so, I'm out of here. See you tomorrow at Whidbey. We'll keep your picture on the piano."

"Rog, Seven. I'm fine. See you tomorrow. Oh, if you've got a screwdriver on you, throw it down so I can get the clock out of this baby." I acknowledged his transmission, knowing by its jocular tone that he really *was* all right.

We headed north, now a flight of seven Corsairs. We landed safely fifty minutes later to the warm welcome of the naval air station. Our maintenance support team had arrived earlier by marine transport and was there to park us. The bewildered crew chief for Jim's aircraft, like a mother hen without her chick, had to hear what we knew of the crash story. Then we repaired to the "O" club to speculate on the cause of Black Sheep Eight's engine failure, which meant that he would miss a fine evening in August for our party. Perhaps it was an act of God.

BACK AT SALEM an exciting and certainly dramatic story was unfolding. Jim had done a magnificent job, considering how little had been given to work with. Engine failure on takeoff is every pilot's worst fear. Landing straight ahead after such a failure at low altitude is drilled into every pilot from the first day of flight training. Making a sharp turn in any direction almost certainly will cause a stall, a quick spin, and instant death. Jim had been at about four hundred feet, maybe less, when his engine quit cold. He was headed straight for downtown Salem.

He had made a slight bank to the right, perhaps 20 degrees, immediately leveling his wings. He was now committed to a wheels-up landing straight ahead. As he glided powerless toward an open plowed field, he had maydayed and lined up his final approach to the dirt field. Then, just before touching down, he saw a big farmhouse looming up before him. With insufficient altitude to bank (and die), he kicked hard, right rudder skidding the airplane to the right, just enough to go sliding past the farmhouse to a dusty, dirt-scattering stop. He had seen someone out of the corner of his eye standing beside the front steps of the two-story dwelling. By performing that skidding maneuver he had just missed crashing into the house and killing everybody in it.

After Jim had communicated with the members of his departing flight and climbed down out of the cockpit, he had walked over to the house. Standing in front of the steps a frightened little six-year-old boy was crying. His family was standing behind him on the porch, obviously hesitant and staring unbelievingly at the scene in their front yard.

Jim walked up to the sobbing child and put an arm around him, speaking gently: "I've got a little boy at home just like you. His name is Terry, and I know how you feel. Everything's going to be fine. Could I speak to your daddy?"

The boy stopped crying. Jim then introduced himself to the stunned family. It did not take them very long to realize how lucky they had been and how much skill this young marine aviator had exercised to avoid hitting their home.

The airport manager had arrived on the scene a few minutes after the crash, and Jim negotiated with him for a twenty-four-hour security watch for the downed Corsair. He had then ridden back to the airport in a farmer's truck. Four or five dozen people had gathered at the site, where they could easily visualize the masterful job Jim had done in performing his controlled crash. Several people had insisted on shaking his hand.

A phone call alerted the military authorities to set up the necessary aircraft recovery procedures and the other details needing attention. Laseter placed a call to his wife, assuring her that he was okay and was looking forward to spending a restful night in Salem. He neglected to tell her how close he had come to a disaster. The airport manager then drove him to a hotel downtown. He had checked in attracting remarkably little notice, given that hardly anybody else was wearing a flight suit. The day's activities had proven to be exhausting. Jim went upstairs, showered, and crawled into bed. It was 3:30 in the afternoon.

About three hours later, he awoke quite refreshed and put on his khaki flight suit and fore-and-aft cap. Descending the stairs, he headed for the dining room, located just off the lobby.

It was so crowded he wondered if he would be able to find an empty table. He needn't have worried. As he entered the room looking for the hostess, everyone stood up facing him and clapped. Suddenly, Jim realized they were clapping for him. It was a touching and emotional moment for all. Jim, the big, strong marine pilot, was moved to tears as everyone came forward, eager to shake his hand and express their gratitude. The family who lived in the farmhouse was there with their young son and two other children.

Jim would never forget this day and this unimaginable evening. He did not for one moment regret missing the party at Whidbey Island.

13 The Most Unauthorized Helicopter Ride Ever

NYONE PAYING ATTENTION will have noted that all of the stories thus far have dealt with survival in some way or another. We have seen pilots lost at sea but rescued (I fall into that category). We have observed from armchair safety several forced landings in which survival was a pretty iffy thing. But there is another kind of survival, characteristic of all military services, and it is called *career* survival.

All officers and noncommissioned officers are graded on their performance. In the case of the commissioned officer, substandard performance and/or failure to be promoted twice in a row usually signals the cashing-out of the individual or forced retirement, depending on the rank and number of years in the service.

What must a Marine Corps career officer do to be terminated before reaching retirement status? Besides the obvious things, such as selling U.S. secrets to a foreign power or deserting one's post in time of war, there are several actions that are seriously frowned upon. For example, it is considered bad taste to punch out a general officer or, for that matter, any officer senior to oneself. One is not allowed to strike an enlisted man for any reason, although General Patton did it. (Allowances may be made for a four-star general, but, as even he found out, it is not a smart thing to do.) A marine officer can lose his weapon, but it had better be lost in twelve thousand feet of ocean, 760 miles at sea. Taking one's girlfriend up for a joy ride in a government airplane might result in an official reprimand. However, should one crash with her on board, that's a sure ticket to a civilian job, assuming one is unfortunate enough to survive.

There are too many ways to become cross-threaded in the military to itemize them all, but the tale told here is a good example of jeopardy and recovery in the process of surviving as a career marine pilot. The attentive reader will note an emphasis on luck more than on skill in this as in other survival stories. In the struggle to stay afloat in a military organization, the luckiest can easily be mistaken for the fittest.

In the military it is impossible to overestimate the power of authorization—proper authorization, no authorization, even nonauthorization (if there were such a word). On every military base, particularly aviation posts, there are two signs that show up everywhere: NO SMOKING and AUTHORIZED PERSONNEL ONLY. The first is pretty understandable, particularly when there is a lot of high-octane gasoline around. The other sign is equally ubiquitous: it is posted at officers quarters, enlisted quarters, security areas, weapons storage areas, and even in the hangars where our own aircraft are parked. Many military people spend their entire careers not really sure whether or not they are fully authorized to be where they are or to do what they're doing. Unfortunately, it's like pregnancy; you are or you are not. Most officers resolve the dilemma by going about their duties in the assumption that they are fully authorized for everything but the Waves' shower room. They can be wrong.

Rolling the calendar back to November, 1953—perhaps the 24th. I say "perhaps" because, even after forty-six years, they might still be investigating this flight, and prudence dictates that I throw them off the track.

The unit, HMR-361, was a marine squadron of transport helicopters located at the Marine Corps air facility at Santa Ana, California. About three months before, I had finished my transition from flying the F2H Banshee and the F9F Panther Jet to flying helicopters. I was a junior captain in the regular establishment and still a little hurt that a competent, fairly hot jet pilot like myself should be snatched from the jaws of glory and reduced to the agony of hovering under some noisy rotor blades. The glamour of high flight had been replaced by the thrill of being able to fly backward.

THE BUSINESS OF helicoptering (my word) was still pretty new, with the Korean action demonstrating rather dramatically that moving armed troops short distances was best accomplished by helicopter and not by jeeps and trucks. The armed gun-ship helicopters would come later, but the senior Marine Corps leaders already saw helicopters in terms of battlefield tactics. Soon it became necessary to staff the many new squadrons, not just with new pilots fresh out of helicopter training, but with combat-experienced pilots, captains and majors.

My bleating of "Why me?" to the detail officer at headquarters fell on deaf ears. I was ordered to Ellyson Field, Pensacola, Florida, to a sixty-hour transition syllabus. The helicopter represents a totally different type of flying, a complete change from jets, and it was a real challenge. Although flying helicopters was certainly better than a ground job and not flying at all, it was more than a year before I admitted to my civilian and Marine Corps friends that I was a helicopter pilot. When asked, "What are you flying now?" I would just say that I was a professional killer on a secret assignment. It always ended the conversation. Besides, it was partly true. I was a professional, and I might screw up and kill myself at any time.

In good ol' HMR-361 (H means helicopter, M stands for marine, and R signifies transport) the daily routine was pointed toward logging flight time and gaining experience in the Sikorsky-made HRS-1. Earlier models of this fine company's efforts were used for pilot rescue in Korea and had definitely proven the value of rotary aircraft. The HRS-1 had seats for about ten troops down in the tunnel (cabin), while the pilot and copilot sat up above in their cockpit, some six or seven feet above. They could not see down into the tunnel and relied on the crew chief for information during troop loadings and debarkings. During external lifts, his eyes and guidance were indispensable.

The HRS-1 was in the developmental stage. The engines in 1953–55 were very underpowered and were several years behind the airframe improvements. In summer weather there was never a seating problem when carrying marines. Only four combat-equipped men could be lifted, so there were plenty of seats to go around. The crew chief usually had to be left behind to work on his tan or whatever they do when not flying.

During external load lifting, the copilot's chief duty (he was excused from making coffee) was to be at the ready to pickle off an external load, should the pilot detect a loss of rotor turns (lifting capability) and need to jettison the load, or crash. Dumping cargo is not such a big deal when practicing around home base with cement blocks, but the ground marines sometimes exhibited a poor sense of humor when we were forced to drop their howitzers and/or ammunition. In later years, with improved lifting power, we could really put the ground guys in a bad mood because we could pickle off such items as mobile radar units, small vehicles, and even medium tanks. They make a wonderful splash when dropped over water that is as hard to describe as it is to explain afterwards. But that's another story.

Our fine helo squadron had a few problems. It was strictly a training outfit; pilots and crewmen came in, flew a certain number of syllabus hours, and went out, usually to Korea. Morale was just above that in a terminal cancer ward. There was always a small faction of pilots who were leaving the service shortly. Everyone has heard of a short-timer's attitude, and classic examples abounded in HMR-361. Flying four hops a day was not all that popular. There were, as we diligent career types saw it, a lot of so-called sea gulls in our squadron; you had to throw rocks at them to get 'em to fly.

On the brighter side of things, there were very few ground duties, the bane of all flying personnel. I don't think I even had a job. We flew and flew, and then flew some more. The goal was to become a helicopter aircraft commander, or HAC, before going to Korea. (I had received notification of impending orders to return to Korea for a second combat tour.) An HAC is the equivalent of a captain on an airline, except that in the marines there is no pay differential between captain and copilot if they were of the same rank. The HAC is the boss and receives the designation after so many hours of total flight time plus qualification in the particular type of helicopter. I remember the HAC syllabus required about sixty hours in-type in all of the facets of helo operations.

In an effort to attain this lofty designation, it was often necessary to fly on weekends—usually only on Saturday for married men like me; Sundays were generally non-duty days. On this particular Saturday I was scheduled for a cross-country training flight to a landing point of my choice, and return. My regular copilot was attending to some serious bachelor duties over the weekend in San Diego. The schedule board assignment read: TOOKER/SCROGGS A/C NO. 13." I did not like the setup. Number 13 is not known for its lucky connotation, and I had seen Scroggs around the ready room several times and was sure I wouldn't like him. Nothing like an open mind to start off a long cross-country training flight together.

Scroggs was a first lieutenant, old for his age, as he had come up through the enlisted ranks. But this had nothing to do with my unfair prejudice. It was his weird looks. He was short and heavily built and had excessive body hair. His nickname was "Smiley," incongruously bestowed because he never smiled. Actually, whenever he opened his mouth slightly, he looked like a boxer with his mouthpiece still in. I was to learn that my assigned copilot had a sense of humor modeled on that of Pontius Pilate. The most flattering thing you could say about "Smiley" was that he had a firm grip on the obvious.

We filed our VFR (Visual Flight Plan) for Santa Barbara, California. We would not need to refuel, as the total estimated flying time would only be around two and one-half hours. We planned to land for coffee and a rest stop at the airport, located in Goleta (now the site of UCSB), twelve miles north of Santa Barbara, where I had graduated from the University of California, Santa Barbara, College in June 1950, a month before being recalled to active duty.

Duly authorized—the operative word—to fly toward my alma mater, I had been planning for weeks to add some entertainment to the flight. Unbeknownst to anyone, copilot and crew chief included, I had made contact with a former roommate and fraternity brother (and president), Robert Anderson, currently in the ROTC at Santa Barbara. Andy had been a radarman third class in World War II and had served for eleven months on the USS *Sitko Bay*, a small carrier escort. Up to now his best aviation story concerned the way the *Sitko Bay*'s AA batteries blew up a kamikaze just short of its hitting the ship, raining parts of enemy engine, fuselage, and pilot all over the flight deck.

We were still good friends, and I was looking forward to demonstrating the finer points of the Sikorsky helicopter to my fraternity brother. All the details had been worked out on the telephone. We would rendezvous on the beach in front of the Mira Mar Hotel.

My only concern was that the helicopter setting down on the beach might alarm some of the hotel guests or nearby residents. Hence, the plan was to touch down, get Andy aboard quickly, and move out smartly. After a brief visit at the airport, I would return him safely to the sands in front of the hotel.

It didn't work out quite that way.

Meanwhile, in an effort to effect some sort of conversation as we flew along, I asked Smiley how he liked helicopters. He said he didn't. Was he going overseas? He didn't know. What was he going to do when he completed his military service? Same response. I was almost startled when he eventually asked, "How about you, Captain? I mean, when you get out of the service?"

Recovering from my surprise at his verbosity, I hit him with one of my favorite "sure-to-get-a-laugh" responses: "Oh, I'm thinking of becoming the public relations director for the Federal Witness Protection Program . . . " (letting this sink in) "except I don't know where to send a resume."

He stared at me briefly, then, realizing I'd made a funny,

showed me his patented mouthpiece smile. We rode in silence the rest of the way.

As we approached Ventura and then Summerland, I told the crew chief in the tunnel below, knowing Smiley would also be listening, "Sergeant, we'll be picking up a passenger on the beach ahead. He'll be standing in front of the hotel on the sand. Help him in quickly. I don't want to be on the ground more than a few seconds. Don't want anyone to think it's an emergency landing or anything."

"Yessir, Captain. I'll be ready."

"Roger. After he's aboard, put that spare headset on him and show him how to use the mike."

"Affirmative. Will do." This from the cabin below.

My jolly copilot looked at me curiously but said nothing. I figured that he deserved a thorough briefing.

"Smiley, we're picking up an army second lieutenant." His nod was barely perceptible.

We flew along the white sandy beach at the edge of the surf line. It was a perfect day to pick up an authorized ROTC person. The hotel came into view along with our solitary passenger, who was standing exactly at the pre-briefed spot. I waved to him out the cockpit window as he responded with a warm and welcome wave in return. My approach was on the money. We flared briefly and set down lightly on the hard-packed sand.

"Wave him over, Sergeant."

"I am, Sir. He's coming."

"Tell him to hurry! Grab him and help him in. I wanna get outta here." No answer from below, but I could see the backside of Andy as he tumbled into the tunnel. I applied full collective and we lifted off immediately and headed for the Santa Barbara airport.

"I'm putting on his headset, Sir . . . OK, he's all set."

Following the pilot's orders precisely, the crew chief waves to a prospective passenger to hurry up and get aboard.

"Thanks, Sarge. Hi, Andy. You were right on time. How do you like this rotary flying?" I knew it was his first helicopter experience. No answer.

"Hope the crew chief wasn't too rough on you, but I didn't want to alarm the hotel residents." Still silence.

"Andy, can you hear me all right? Crew chief, does he know how to work the mike?"

"Yes, Sir, he's hearing you."

Finally, our passenger punched the mike button. "I hear you, Sir, but my name is David."

I was suddenly in shock! Who was David? If he wasn't Andy, why the hell did he get into my helicopter?

"Your name is David?" I asked, hoping Andy was having his little joke. I could not see the compartment below and, of course, couldn't ask the crew chief if our new passenger was Robert Anderson, the two never having met.

"Yes, Sir." At least he was polite.

"OK, David," I began, sweating somewhat. "Why did you get into my helicopter?"

"Well, Sir, you waved at me and when you landed, your man in the cabin motioned me over. I thought maybe you were in some sort of trouble. And when I came up alongside, your guy grabbed me and threw me in."

"Holy shit!" I announced over the intercom, "A-ah, David, there's been a little mix-up here."

I was groping for an explanation of any kind. Smiley was a lot of help, if staring is any help. My brain re-engaged for a moment. If David, after he was returned to the beach pickup point, blurted out his aerial kidnapping to his folks, his friends, the newspapers, and then the radio, even the Marine Corps commandant . . . my career would be over. Curtains. What if we crashed? All negative thoughts. Must come up with something.

"David, it's like this: I really shouldn't be telling you this, but if you'll promise not to say anything to anyone, I'll brief you on our mission."

"Oh, yes, Sir; I understand. I won't say a word."

"Good boy, David." From his voice I judged him to be about fourteen, maybe fifteen years old. I could practically smell the aroma of a court-martial.

"David, we're on a special mission from a navy carrier offshore. We were to pick up a special agent from almost the exact spot where you were standing. He must have met with foul play. If I were you, I wouldn't hang around here very long . . . you never know. We have an alternate pickup spot north of here. You realize I can't tell you where; but if you were to let out word of this mission, something might happen to the special agent, or even us." The copilot's mouth was ajar.

"So, David, give me your word you'll not break our trust, OK?"

"Oh, I won't, Sir. . . ." There was a brief quiet period while I negotiated a second approach, flare, and landing on the firm sands of the Mira Mar Beach Hotel.

"I enjoyed the ride, Sir." David was grateful for certain. I could only pray he believed my wild, conjured-up "secret mission" story.

Once he was clear of the chopper, we lifted up and away. He waved briefly and then dashed off into some trees. Handing over the controls to my unwilling accomplice, I took some deep breaths and sank down into my seat.

We landed at the Santa Barbara airport without further incident. So far, so good. While the copilot and crew chief had coffee and a roll, I made for the nearest pay phone. I reached an apologetic ROTC candidate. His car wouldn't start, and there was no way to reach me once airborne, so he had remained at home. I told him it was okay, no problem, sorry he missed the ride. As for the pseudo-kidnapping—well, he could hear about that later.

As we prepared to crank up our "No. 13," which by now more than substantiated my feeling that thirteen is indeed an unlucky number, I gave my crew another thorough briefing.

"Let's head home. Our passenger couldn't make it . . . held up on official business, I guess." The sergeant nodded his understanding and stood by with a fire bottle for an engine startup. Smiley didn't smile; he just climbed up the copilot's side of the helicopter. Apparently, they both figured I was acting properly, even if a little out of the ordinary. Anyway, it was my responsibility as captain of the ship; right or wrong, *they* were in the clear.

The flight back was as serene as the flight up had been stressful. First Lieutenant Scroggs was a smoldering hotbed of apathy all the way back to MCAF Santa Ana. The best I could come up with to explain his incuriosity was that he must have believed my secret-agent tale, although that bit of reasoning didn't hold water. The only other plausible explanation was that he just didn't give a rat's ass.

EPILOGUE

To date, nothing has ever come of my bending the rules of both career survival and authorization. Of course, the brothers in Santa Barbara had an enormous laugh when I finally relayed the incident to Andy.

Besides the Marine Corps and my flight crewmen, I owe a huge apology to my surprised kidnappee. So, David, if you're out there, it's safe now; the "secret mission" has been cancelled. Call me; I'm in the book. . . .

14 A Rescue Mission Gone Bad

The hero of this story will be familiar to readers of chapters 4 and 6. Ken Reusser started off his combat career by shooting down a Japanese bomber, ditching his fighter near Guadalcanal, and being rescued by friendly natives. Later, in 1945, as a captain flying Corsairs out of Okinawa, he got away with chewing up portions of a Japanese reconnaissance plane, in the air, with his aircraft's propeller. By the time of the Korean War, when I met him, he had already accumulated enough medals and honors for a lifetime—but there were more to come.

Ken Reusser is one active "take-it-to-'em" guy, as I know from my own experience in Korea in 1950. Ken was a major in the regular Marine Corps establishment, and I was a reserve first lieutenant. We were flying Corsairs out of Wonsan (K-25) and later Yongpo (K-27) with the difficult mission assigned of covering the strategic withdrawal of army and Marine Corps units at the Chosin Reservoir.

Our unit was the legendary VMF-214 Black Sheep Squadron. Upon joining VMF-214, I was assigned by chance to Ken's division of four aircraft. After our first mission, I was permanently scheduled to fly on his wing, at Ken's request, although I did not know it at the time.

He liked to fly under trees and below rooftops while searching for enemy troops, tanks, and trucks, and that suited me fine. My previous flight leaders were somewhat more reluctant, to put it diplomatically, to get down that low. Looking back now, I'm not so sure that our boldness was of Phi Beta Kappa stuff—maybe it was even of the wrong stuff.

But Ken and I were able to locate and usually destroy considerable amounts of enemy equipment when other flights had reported no enemy activity. My admiration for his leadership reached a high point on one mission in particular when we spotted a lot of supplies on sleds with runners. Sometimes men, but usually horses, were used to transport such loads. On a second dry run for identification we located forty or fifity horses corralled in some burned-out buildings nearby. As we rolled in to our firing run, Ken radioed simply, "Not a good target. Save your ammo. Join up and we'll head north for another look." I don't know to this day if I could have strafed those "enemy" horses, but thanks to Ken, I didn't have to find out.

We flew twelve more missions together in Korea, often just the two of us. For some reason, some of the other pilots viewed our low-altitude search methods with a cool eye. But our aircraft were never once hit by enemy ground fire, perhaps because we were in and out quickly, or maybe we were just too low for the enemy troops to make suitable elevation adjustments.

After the evacuation at Hungnam during that December, our paths separated. Ken went aboard the carrier USS Sicily, and I joined another marine squadron aboard the

USS Bataan. We never flew together again, but the story that he brought with him from the Vietnam War, told here, is as vivid to me as though I had been there. I know his style. Now for the telling of it.

THE VIETNAM WAR was into its third year and several things were obvious: First, under the prevailing rules of engagement, which allowed the enemy a sanctuary, victory was not just around the corner. Second, the North Vietnamese / Vietcong soldiers were not dumb, nor were they easy to fight. Masters at camouflage, they often chose the time and place to fight. Their specialty, if you could call it that, was the ambush. By observing the U.S. forces' methodology and habits, they were able to surprise small infantry units on patrol or even larger forces protected from above by fixed-wing aircraft and armed helicopters.

The VC were particularly fond of setting traps for downed U.S. helicopters. They knew that the U.S. forces always tried to recover not only downed pilots and crewmen but their helicopter as well if it were not damaged beyond salvage-ability.

Such circumstances made for graphic and violent stories, of which this is one. It is most unfortunately true—but good luck plays a briefly brilliant role in it.

IT WAS 14 DECEMBER 1966, in Danang, South Vietnam. The day before, a CH-46 had been shot down during a medical evacuation. As the chopper flew at a thousand feet over an area reported to be reasonably quiet, a sudden burst of gunfire from the jungle below had damaged both jet engines and had resulted in an autorotation and forced landing on a reasonably flat, grassy area the size of a football field. The six-man crew had been picked up by an accompanying CH-46

A Marine CH-46 in Vietnam, circa 1967, lands in tall grass to discharge combat troops. *U.S. Marine Corps*

transport helicopter and returned safely to Marble Mountain (in the general Danang area).

Next day the MAG-16 (Marine Air Group) commanding officer, Col. Ken Reusser, met with the wing commander, Major General Robertshaw. They decided to attempt the extraction (pickup) of the downed bird, which was less than fifty miles from their headquarters. The weather was marginal, but the distance was not a problem and rescue facilities were available. The tactical consequences of losing a helicopter, along with its dollar value of almost $1.5 million, were influential in the decision.

Later in the war there would be giant heavy-lift helicopters, capable of lifting empty CH-46s. But in 1966 flying cranes were not yet readily available. Instead, recovering a helicopter had evolved into a businesslike but deadly dangerous procedure. First, a ground security force of infantry was heli-lifted into the area adjacent to the downed helicopter. These troops were covered from above by helicopter gun ships, normally by the branch of service that had suffered the loss of the crashed helo. If the ground security commander felt, after a thorough reconnaissance, that the extraction could be carried out with a "reasonable" degree of safety, the mission went forward. If not, the mission was scrubbed after destroying the downed aircraft. (Note: Helicopters are considered to be aircraft.)

Accordingly, a second CH-46 was dispatched to the site with a special maintenance crew aboard to dismantle the downed aircraft. They would remove the rotor blades, engines, transmissions, gearboxes, and anything else necessary to reduce the overall weight, thus making the helicopter hulk liftable by another CH-46.

This retracting helo was a special, one-of-a-kind bird. It had been stripped of every item not absolutely essential for flight. Even the fuel was loaded with just enough for the round trip. It was nicknamed the "Stake" for no known reason except perhaps that it was considered a stakeout, as in "sitting duck." It was just that, as we shall see.

Once the dismantlers had done their job, the Stake would be called in. The grounded helo was now liftable, and the ground defense forces had taken defensive positions to support the extraction.

To further ensure success, airborne helicopter gun ships were assigned to patrol the peripheral areas. On this occasion, General Robertshaw suggested that Ken Reusser fly to the rescue scene with one of the gun ships and make an on-site evaluation, taking into account the many factors involved, not the least of which was the weather. Ken would fly in the copilot's seat, the left side, and operate the forward firing 7.62-mm machine guns and rockets, if necessary. He would otherwise be free to man the UHF radios while orbiting the crash scene, as senior officer present. The pilot in command of the UH-IE was Capt. Leon Chadwick, from Raleigh, North Carolina, who was only twenty-six years old but was an experienced helicopter pilot. The two crewmen who manned the swivel-mounted 7.62-mm guns from their cabin side mounts were Sgt. Dan Bennett, the crew chief, and Cpl. Rodolfo Gonzales, the gunner.

"You know where we're headed, Captain?" Ken asked.

"Yes, Sir, Happy Valley." The marines had so named this reputedly dangerous valley as their way of belittling the fact that quite a few of their helicopters had been shot down or hit while traversing its boundaries. Yet when substantial ground forces had gone into the valley to dispose of the threat, they had found only a few water buffalo and lots of smelly rice paddies.

"Got your gloves, Colonel?" the captain asked.

"Yeah, thanks." Ken reached into a pocket of his flight suit and extracted two woeful-looking summer flying gloves that looked like solid blobs of modeling clay. The sweat from previous missions had corroded them into an unwearable condition.

"I'll have to survey these awful things," Ken said with a smile. "Nothing stays dry out here for long." Ken could not know how important *not* wearing gloves would be . . . for the rest of his life. Then both pilots concentrated on their duties as they proceeded to the coordinates of the downed and now stripped helicopter.

With Chadwick at the controls and the colonel on the radio, the twenty-minute flight went smoothly. Both crewmen had inserted the 30-caliber ammo belts in their M-60c machine guns, ready for any hand that might be dealt.

Ken pressed the mike button on the cyclic stick: "This is

Charlie Victor One, have area in sight. Come in, Ground Unit."

"Roger, Charlie Victor One, this is Fire Team 14. Have you in sight. Our CP is about five hundred yards due south of the downed helo. Everything's been quiet so far. We've got three half-tracks, two jeeps, some six-bys, and an ambulance. We've borrowed a couple of 50-calibers just in case." The ground element had checked in.

"A-ah, Roger, Fire Team 14. Break . . . Stake aircraft, I believe I have you west of the site, is that you?"

"Affirm, Charlie Victor. We're up here at five grand, cooling down. The weather's opened up in just the last fifteen, twenty minutes. We're ready to come down and go to work, iff'n you say so."

The informality of the Stake chopper's crew was an understandable antidote to high tension. Once they came in to hoist out the wreck, they were literally sitting ducks. One of their pilots at a recent happy hour said, "It was like being at a church social with your pants down and not being able to pull them up."

"Charlie Victor One, this is Best Man 26. We're a flight of four Huey gun ships inbound to your position. We're about five minutes out. Request instructions."

"OK, this is Charlie Victor. Looks like we've got a plan here. The weather's given us a break, the ground people are in place, and no one has reported any enemy fire. So as soon as Best Man gets here, let's move 'em out. I'll say when."

"Almost too quiet," Ken said on the intercom. Both gunners nodded their agreements, as did the young captain.

"I hope the gun ships will influence the VC to stay in their hooches, Sir," said the captain. Ken nodded, as the four Hueys arrived and took up their circling pattern around the site.

"OK, guys, this is Charlie Victor. Let's get it done. Stake Chopper, come on down; we'll cover you." Ken nodded to his pilot to descend to a lower altitude so as to observe from a closer viewpoint.

"We'll fly shotgun, Captain," and to the gunners in the rear of the cabin, "Stay alert! This is the moment of truth."

The heavy-lift CH-46 came to a hover directly over the stripped helicopter on the ground and lowered its special heavy-duty hoist cable to the two men below, who would attach the cable hooks to the proper lifting eyelets. As the slack was taken up in the hoist cable, both helicopters inched skyward as if in slow motion.

Suddenly there were flashes all over the sides of the Stake chopper.

"This is Stake; we're taking fire, from the high ground just to the east. Feels like 20-mm. They're HEI [high explosive incendiary, a U.S.-made ammunition]!"

"Roger from Charlie Victor. We're directly over that area. I can see smoke coming from their position. We're rolling in." Ken could hear the scary sounds of rounds impacting on the Stake aircraft when the pilot had opened his mike to declare the emergency.

"Switches and gunsight are on, Chadwick. Hold your run steady on that small knoll. They must have fifties there or even some captured twenties of ours."

As the UH-1E raced down to near treetop level, Ken fired all seven rockets from each external pod and pressed the trigger on the forward firing M60s. On the pullout he could hear both gunners firing their weapons.

"I didn't see anything, did you?" Ken asked.

"Negative, they're probably hidden in those trees . . . but good shooting, Colonel."

"This is Stake, we're still catching it. I've pickled off our load [the CH-46]. We're hit a bunch. Still have power. Moving away to the west."

"Roger, Stake. Best Man, do you and your flight have the target in sight? The hill we just hit?"

"Affirmative, Charlie Victor. We're across the valley from you now. We'll roll in about one minute. Saw your rocket hits, is that the target?"

"Yes, but they're still shooting. Should be enough VC to go around," Ken advised. "We're rolling in for a second run."

Captain Chadwick pushed the cyclic stick forward as Ken squinted through the crude but effective ring-and-post sight. The realization that they had flown into an ambush flashed through both their minds. The trap for the helicopter retrieval mission had been sprung, and this time the North Vietnamese had brought along their heavy stuff.

"More to the right toward that hilltop," Ken directed. "Uh-oh, here it comes!" Red and white tracers arced in their direction like fireflies, seemingly harmless.

The Huey rocked and bucked and then lurched into a sickening nose-high attitude. Explosive rounds had hit the helicopter.

"Nose over, nose over," Ken yelled, not bothering with the intercom. Sensing something very wrong, he glanced at the pilot. In horror, he saw that Captain Chadwick had taken an instantly fatal hit. Helmet and head were gone, the blood still pumping. Ken's reaction was revulsive but only momentary. He grabbed the controls and attempted to right the plunging helicopter but both the collective and cyclic were sloppy and unresponsive. Only the rudder actions remained to control the helicopter. As other rounds struck the helicopter, he knew that they would crash. He felt a sting in his left hip much like a BB-gun pellet. (The sting turned out to be a 50-caliber slug that removed about half a pound of flesh.)

The Huey was staggering now, the controls all but useless. Ken could hear the gunners still firing their machine guns, although at what he didn't know. The airspeed indicator showed seventy knots as the helicopter dove earthward in a hard left-hand bank. He could sense that they were on fire and braced himself for the crash.

The aircraft smashed into the ground with an impact so hard that the tail boom sheared just aft of the cabin and catapulted over the top of the cockpit, ending up in front of the aircraft. It resembled an inverted pair of pliers. Ironically, they had crashed against the foot of the high ground that the intense fire had been coming from. So far the only good thing that had happened to this ill-fated flight was that the wreckage was now in defilade (below the sighting angle) of the enemy.

Momentarily stunned, Ken recovered his senses enough to assess his situation. His seat had broken from its mounts on impact, but he was still inside the general remains of the shattered cockpit. He could move everything and felt no pain from his severely damaged thigh. He failed to notice a smaller bullet hole in his right arm just below the elbow. The pilot's seat had been thrown forward under the instrument panel, the captain's body still strapped in it. Ken knew there was nothing to be done there.

The main fuel cell had burst upon impact and the fire was now the governing factor. As Ken struggled to undo his lap and shoulder harness, he heard screams from inside the burning cabin. He was not the only one in danger of being burned alive.

The harness release buckles were apparently jammed and

were holding him prisoner to the oncoming flames. In total desperation, Ken leaned backward toward the fire, only inches away, in hopes of burning through the nylon straps. After a few painful seconds, he lunged forward to see if the straps would give way. They didn't. He repeated this last-chance maneuver again, lunging forward to break the tough nylon webbed belts. After five or six of these painful episodes he was finally free; he knew the flesh that he could smell burning was his.

The screams for help behind him had intensified his efforts to vacate the burning helicopter and get back to the trapped gunners. He rolled over and over on the ground to snuff out the smoldering remnants of his flight suit. Upon regaining his feet, he staggered back into the now raging inferno, a magnesium and aluminum ball of fire fed by jet petroleum fuel.

He could see the legs of one of the crewmen (Sergeant Bennett) protruding slightly from the crumpled, accordion-folded cabin compartment. He reached his gloveless hands into the burning helicopter and tried to move a plexiglass door that seemed to be pinning the crewman inside. It would not budge.

Next, he grabbed the gunner's legs and pulled as hard as he could. Oddly, for some reason he had very little strength, and his efforts were proving to be futile. This fact, he realized later, was due to the severe injuries to his left leg and right arm. The burns had not yet started their painful assault.

The heat was intense and the fire seemed to be everywhere. Out of the corner of his eye, he saw someone running toward him. A huge shape hit him squarely in the midsection, and he went sprawling on the ground. A giant navy corpsman then picked him up like a sack of potatoes and stumbled away from the burning helicopter.

Colonel Reusser attempts, unsuccessfully, to free a trapped crew member from his UH-1E helicopter. Two CH-46s are under enemy fire in the background. *painting by Alex Durr*

As they reached a point no more than fifty feet away, they heard a loud "whoosh" followed by an explosion, and the helicopter blew up, raining parts everywhere. Ken was alive by only a matter of seconds. The corpsman had realized that there was no time for discussion with the pilot in the smoldering flight suit who was apparently trying to climb back into his burning Huey helicopter.

The navy corpsman was part of the security ground force and had seen the chopper stagger when hit and subsequently crash. He had run through the open field more than three hundred yards, dodging bullets from the enemy's hilltop position.

"What about my crew?" Ken had shouted. The corpsman merely shook his head, confirming what Ken had feared.

"They never had a chance, Sir. And you wouldn't have either if . . . ." They both knew what was unspoken.

Gently dragging the 190-pound pilot to safer quarters, the navy hospitalman removed Ken's helmet, only to find that the Styrofoam lining inside the hard hat had actually melted and the scalding material had run down over Ken's ears and neck. (These scars would never disappear.) He wrapped Ken's left thigh tightly with gauze and then the smaller wound in Ken's right arm. As the medical attention was being administered, the air ground battle on the hill just above them continued.

When complete control and containment were finally achieved, it was almost dark. A half-track vehicle had finally made its way over to Ken's position. He and the corpsman were heli-lifted back to the hospital at Danang. The stripped helicopter was abandoned to the VC; but the Stake CH-46, badly damaged, made it safely home. The cost to the Americans had been severe: Captain Chadwick, Sergeant Bennett, Corporal Gonzales, a member of the Stake helicopter's ground crew, and almost a group commander as well.

At the hospital, Ken's condition was listed as critical and his next of kin notified. He had second- and third-degree burns over 45 percent of his body. The .50-caliber slug (luckily, Ken said) had hit only flesh, missing the femur by less than an

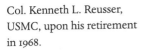

Col. Kenneth L. Reusser, USMC, upon his retirement in 1968.

inch. His hands were horribly burned, almost beyond usability. His back was particularly in bad shape from his repeated leaning into the fire to free himself from the shoulder straps. The doctors cleaned up the burns as best they could, but it was obvious that Ken needed to be air-evacuated to the United States as soon as possible.

Describing the pain of burns such as those incurred by Colonel Reusser is impossible. Only someone similarly burned can truly understand the physical and mental anguish involved. Perhaps an analogy offered by Ken, later in happier times, will help. He said, "Imagine the worst burn you've ever experienced, say, a burned finger or a burn from scalding hot liquid. Then mentally put the equivalent of that pain over half of your body. It still won't exactly describe it, but at least you'll have a good idea."

After several shots of morphine that same night, Ken heard two night-duty corpsmen outside his room discussing (callously, he thought) his prognosis.

"That colonel in there . . . the one that was burned today. He ain't gonna make it, what I hear."

But they didn't know Ken Reusser. He had survived a ditching in the South Pacific, with his left eye hanging by its optical cord for fifteen days. He had flown 213 combat missions in three wars and survived. He would live through this ordeal, too—after undergoing many painful debriding and grafting operations at the Bethesda Naval Hospital in Maryland. He would have to wear hairpieces where his scalp had been scalded by melting Styrofoam, and most of his body would be badly scarred for life.

And he would never give up, living life to its fullest, sometimes to a dangerous extent. His son says, "He doesn't *do* slow," and Ken himself says that he is not ready for the wrecking ball yet.

ABOUT THE AUTHOR

D. K. TOOKER was commissioned and received his navy wings in April 1947. While flying as a "weekend warrior," he attended the University of California, Santa Barbara, graduating in 1950. Recalled to active duty in the Korean War, he logged 133 combat missions. During the course of his service, Colonel Tooker transitioned from jets to helicopters to observation aircraft before returning to jets to fly the F-8 Crusader. His decorations include two Distinguished Flying Crosses, ten Air Medals, two Navy Commendation Medals, and the Presidential Unit Citation. He lives in Orange, California.

The Naval Institute Press is the book-publishing arm of the U.S. Naval Institute, a private, nonprofit, membership society for sea service professionals and others who share an interest in naval and maritime affairs. Established in 1873 at the U.S. Naval Academy in Annapolis, Maryland, where its offices remain today, the Naval Institute has members worldwide.

Members of the Naval Institute support the education programs of the society and receive the influential monthly magazine *Proceedings* and discounts on fine nautical prints and on ship and aircraft photos. They also have access to the transcripts of the Institute's Oral History Program and get discounted admission to any of the Institute-sponsored seminars offered around the country.

The Naval Institute also publishes *Naval History* magazine. This colorful bimonthly is filled with entertaining and thought-provoking articles, first-person reminiscences, and dramatic art and photography. Members receive a discount on *Naval History* subscriptions.

The Naval Institute's book-publishing program, begun in 1898 with basic guides to naval practices, has broadened its scope in recent years to include books of more general interest. Now the Naval Institute Press publishes about one hundred titles each year, ranging from how-to books on boating and navigation to battle histories, biographies, ship and aircraft guides, and novels. Institute members receive discounts of 20 to 50 percent on the Press's more than eight hundred books in print.

Full-time students are eligible for special half-price membership rates. Life memberships are also available.

For a free catalog describing Naval Institute Press books currently available, and for further information about subscribing to *Naval History* magazine or about joining the U.S. Naval Institute, please write to:

Membership Department
U.S. Naval Institute
291 Wood Road
Annapolis, MD 21402-5034
Telephone: (800) 233-8764
Fax: (410) 269-7940
Web address: www.usni.org